PARISNEWYORKPORTRAITS
ASHKAN SAHIHI

PARISNEWYORKPORTRAITS
ASHKAN SAHIHI

Deutscher
Kunstverlag

This book is dedicated to my mother,
the mother of my children,
and the mothers of my grandchildren.

Emily

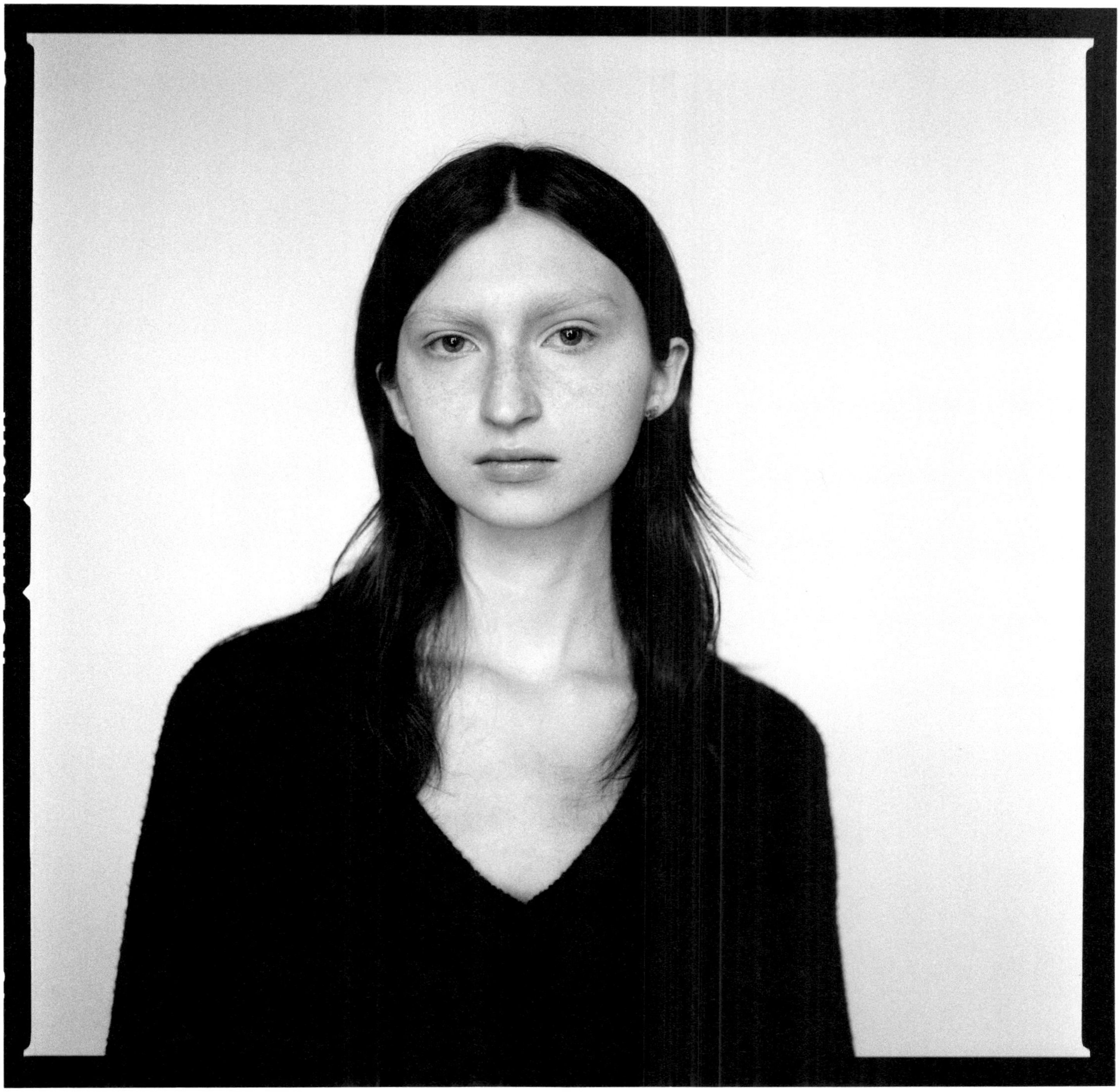

Anyon

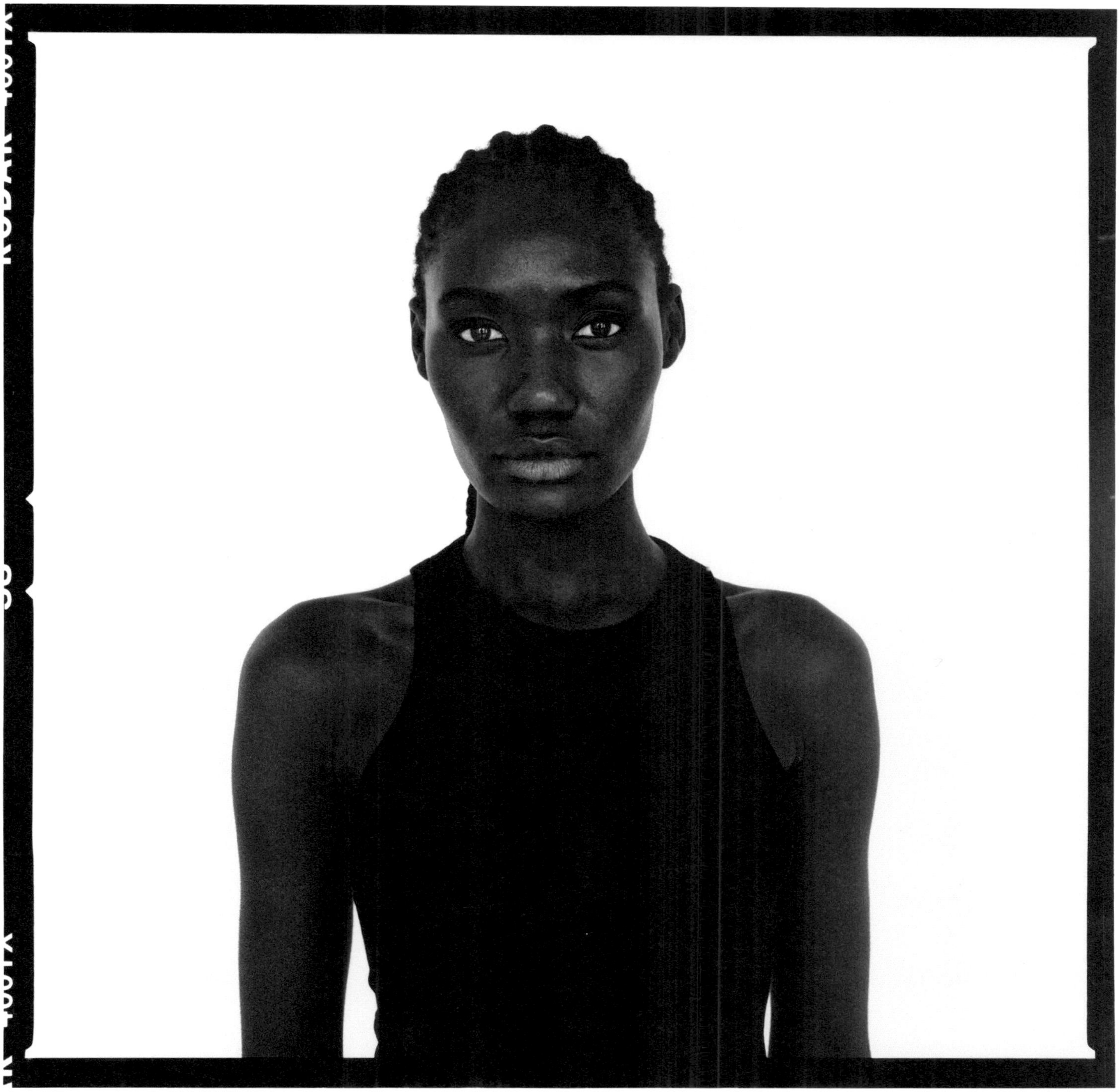

Morgane

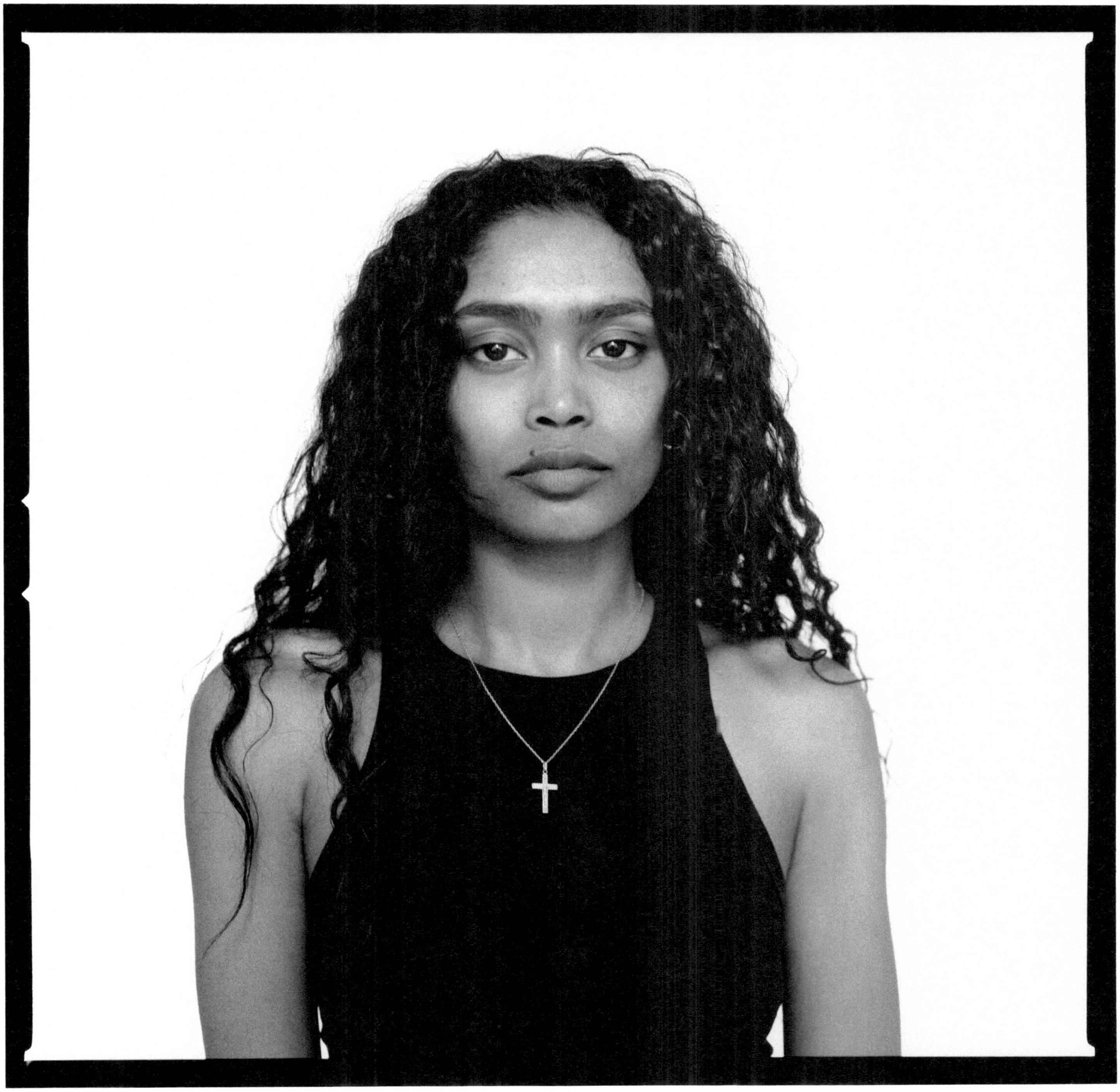

Raysa

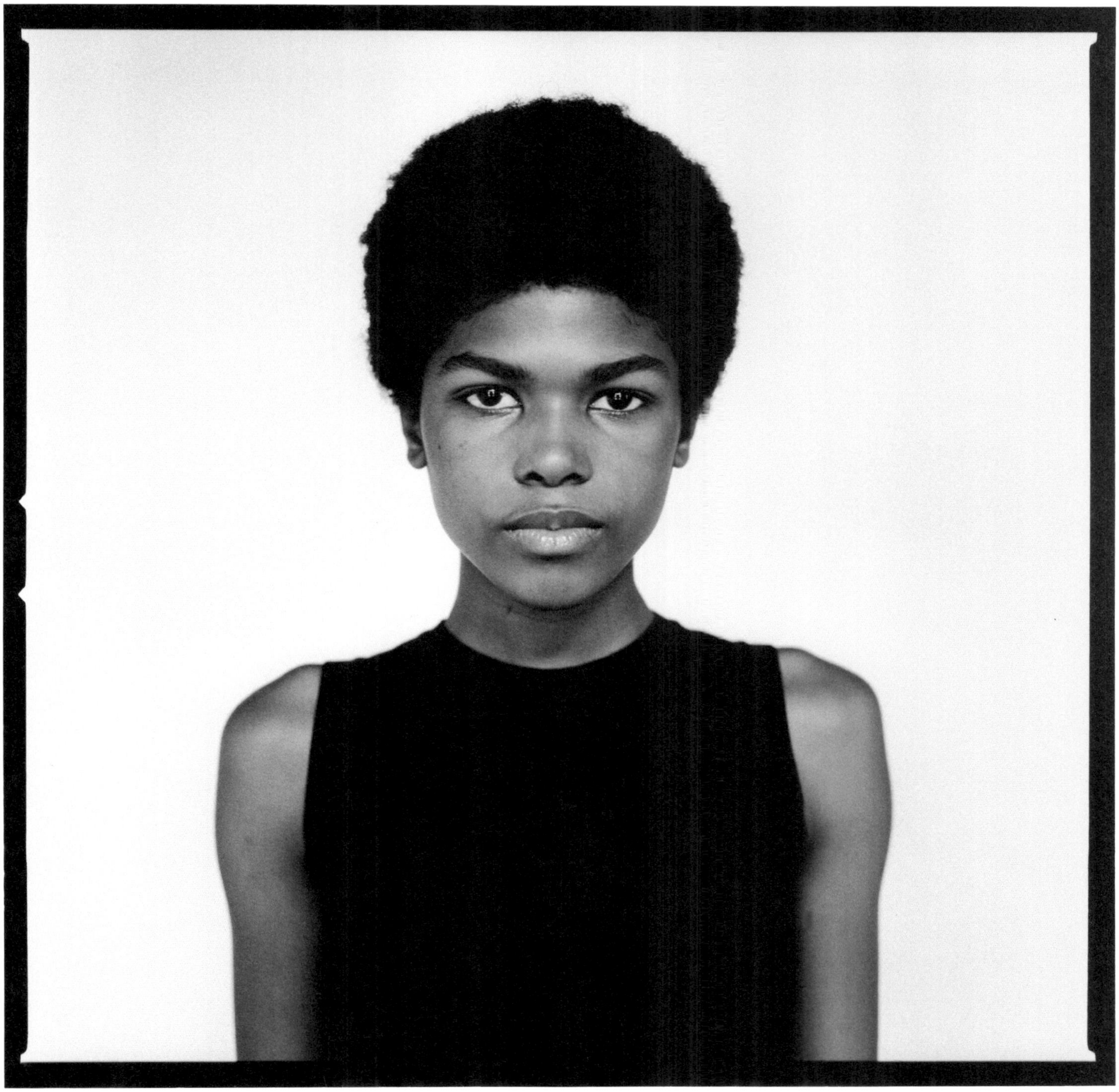

Rayane

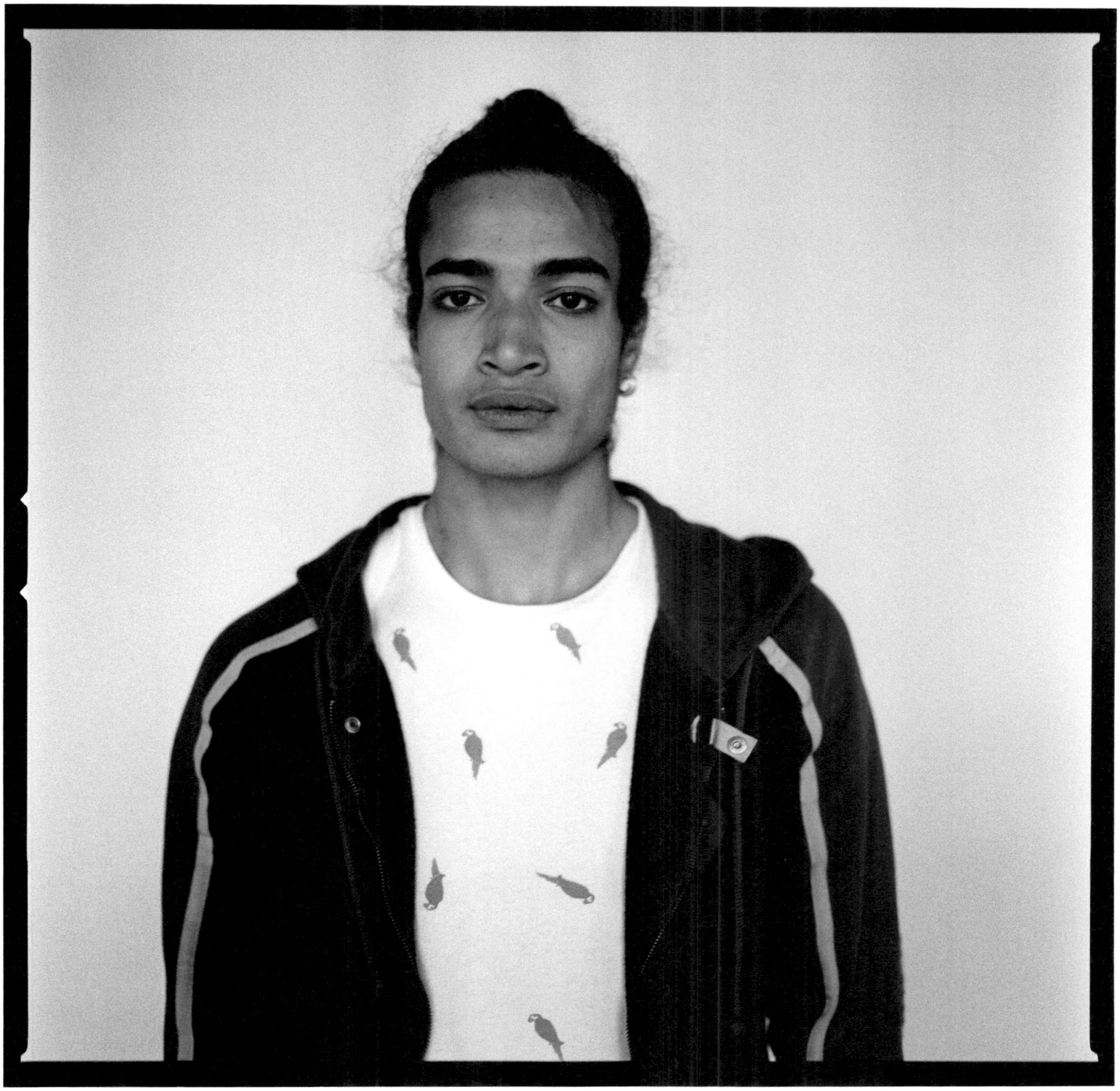

Chen XI

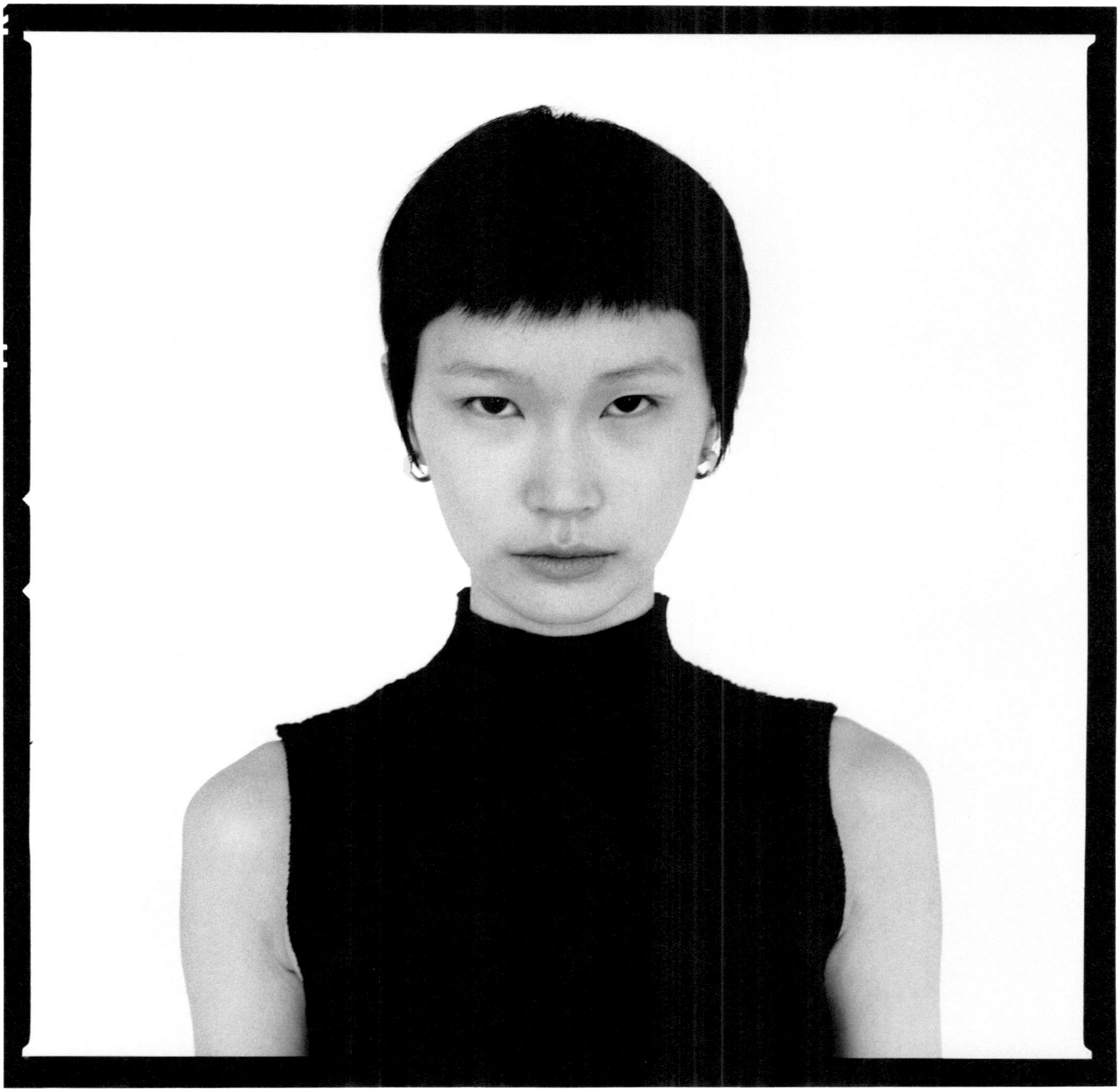

Sydney

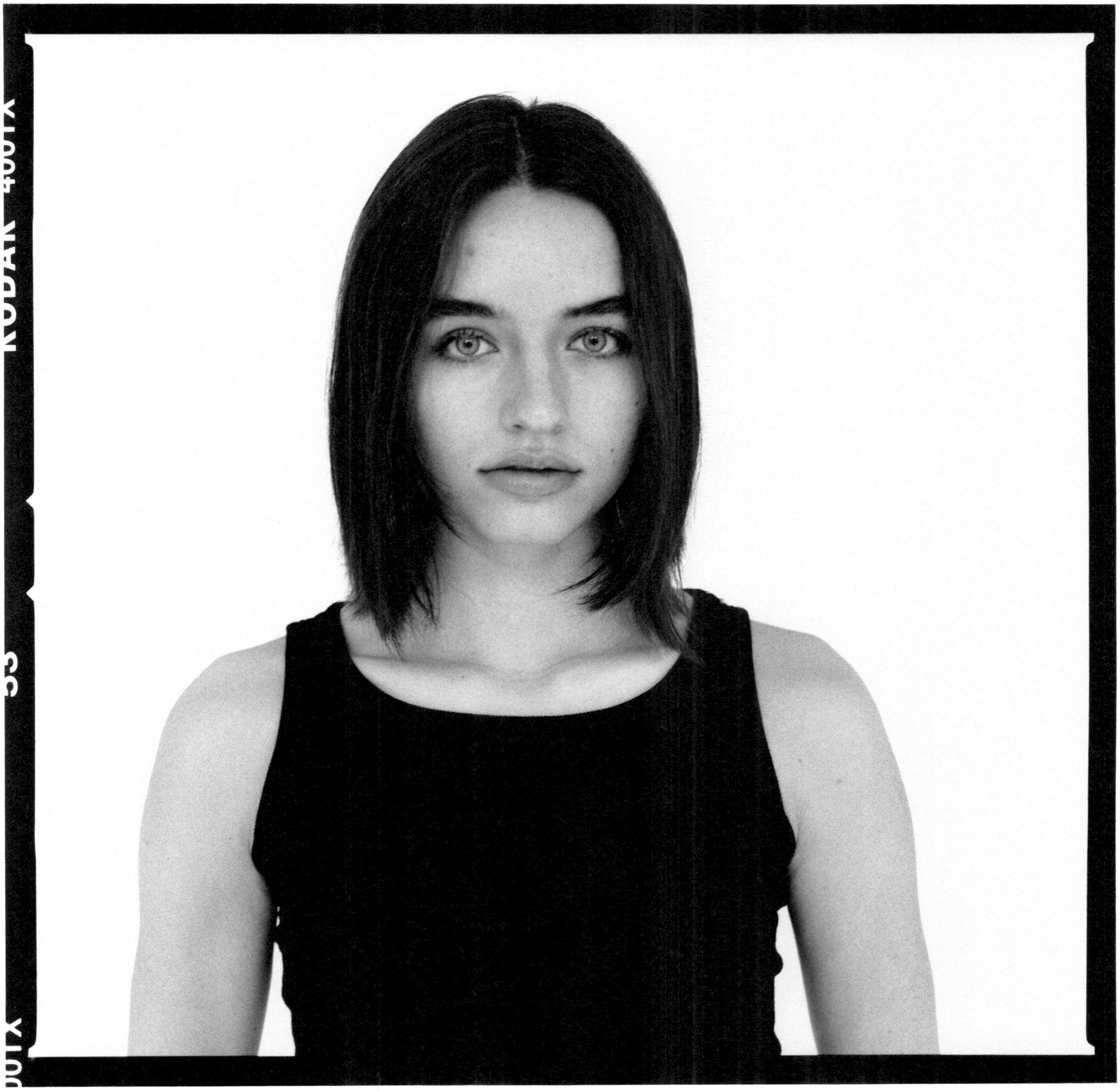
KODAK 400TX
33

Tya

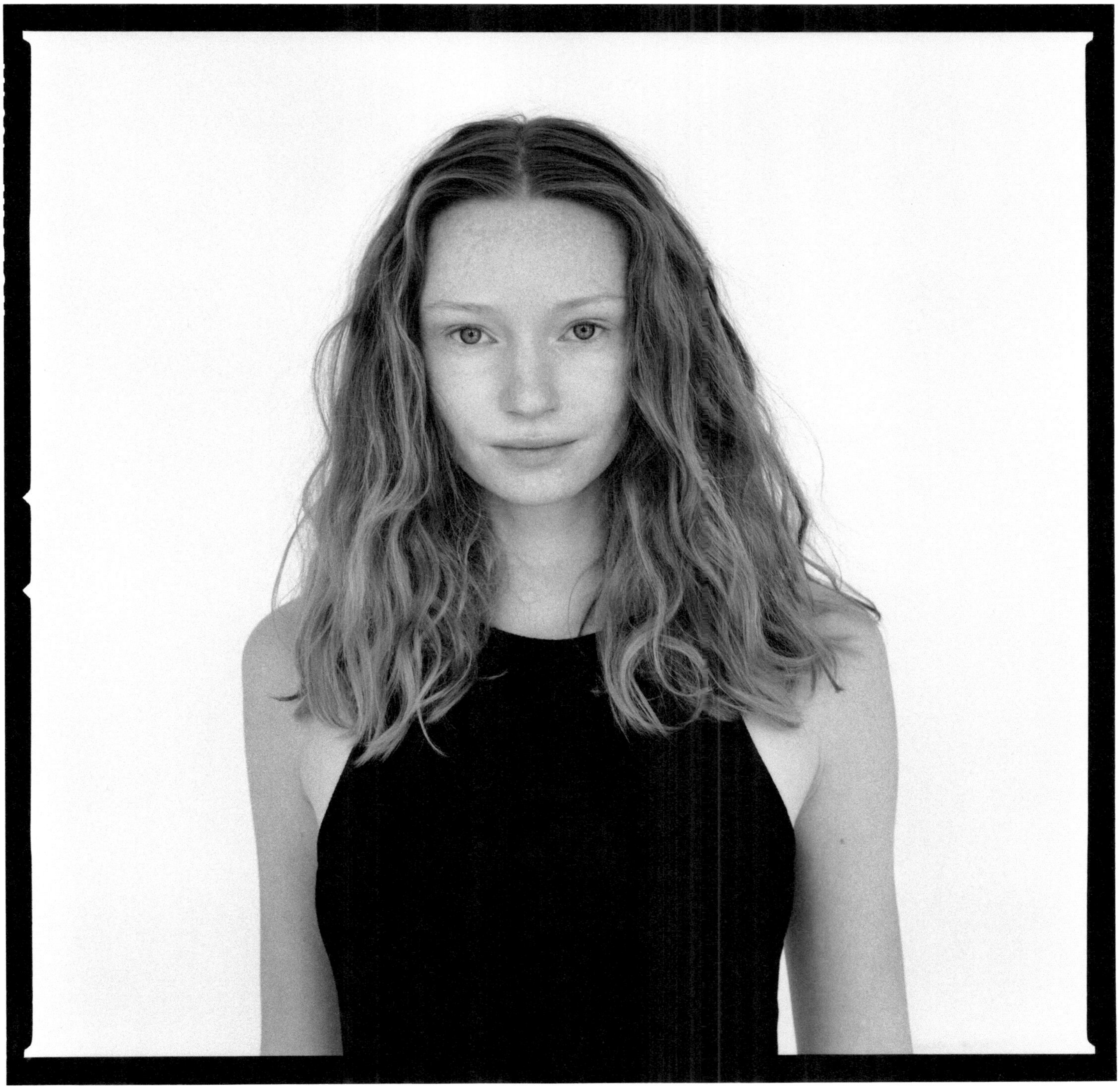

Marisa

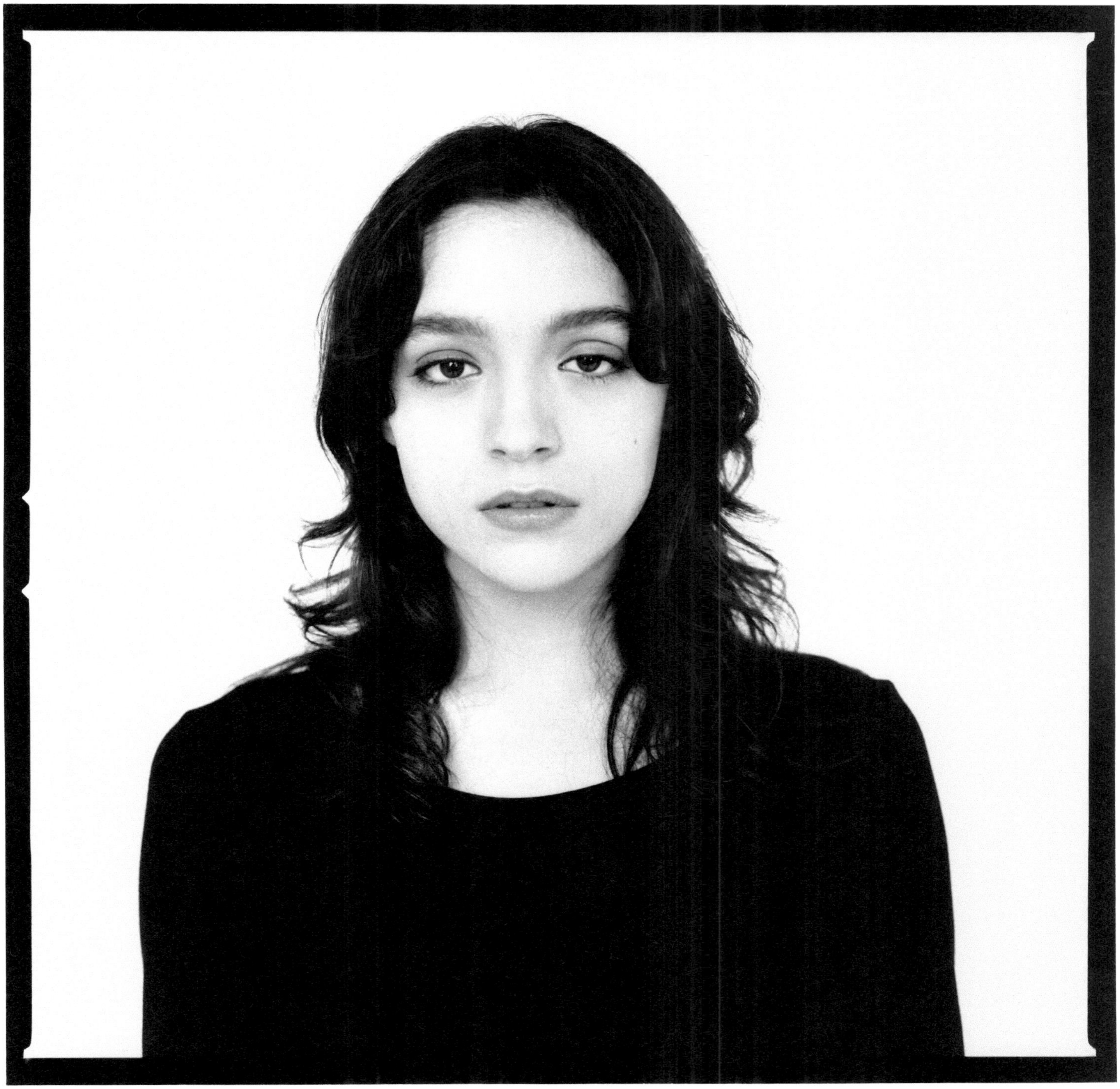

Jake

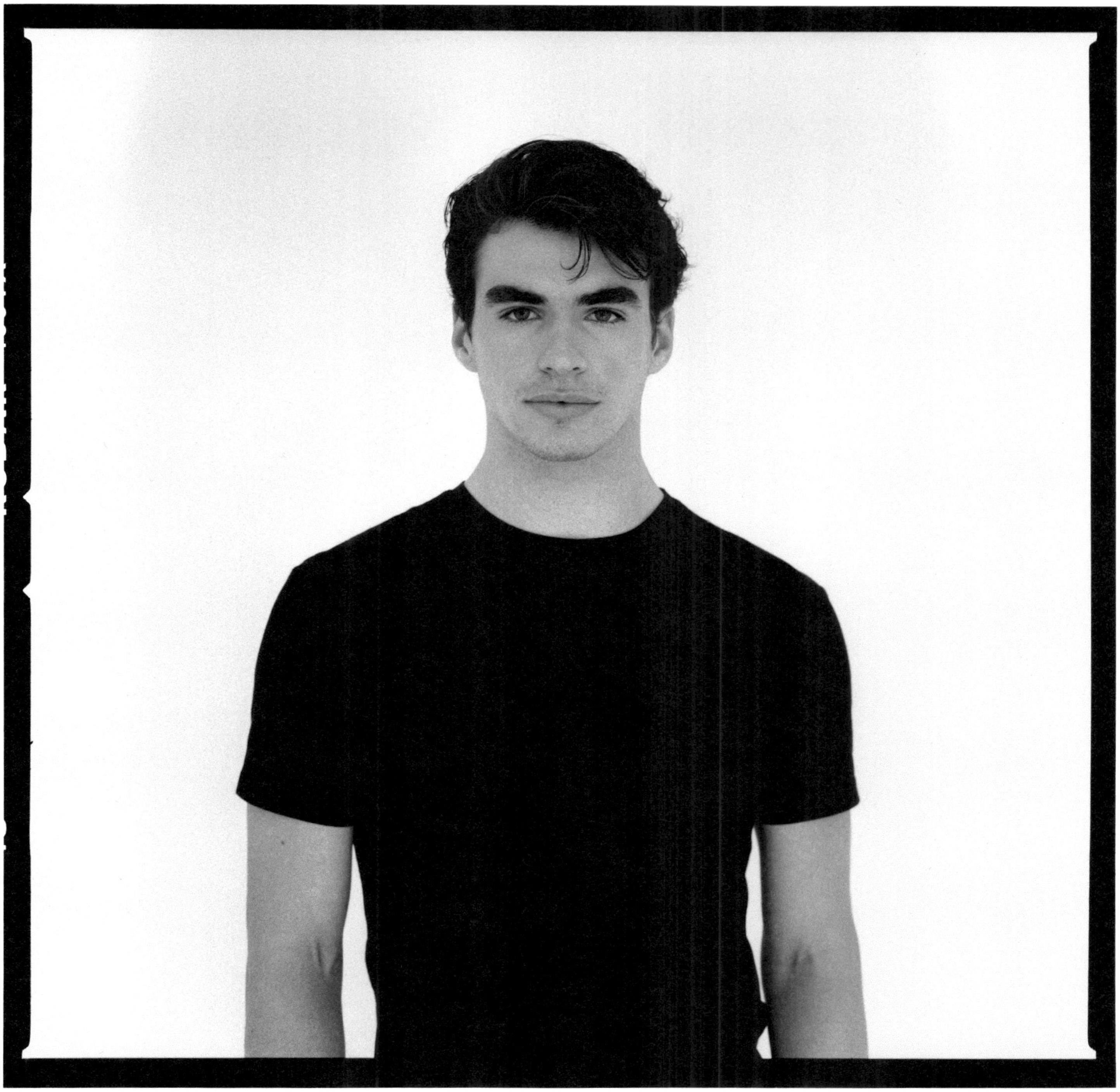

Syd

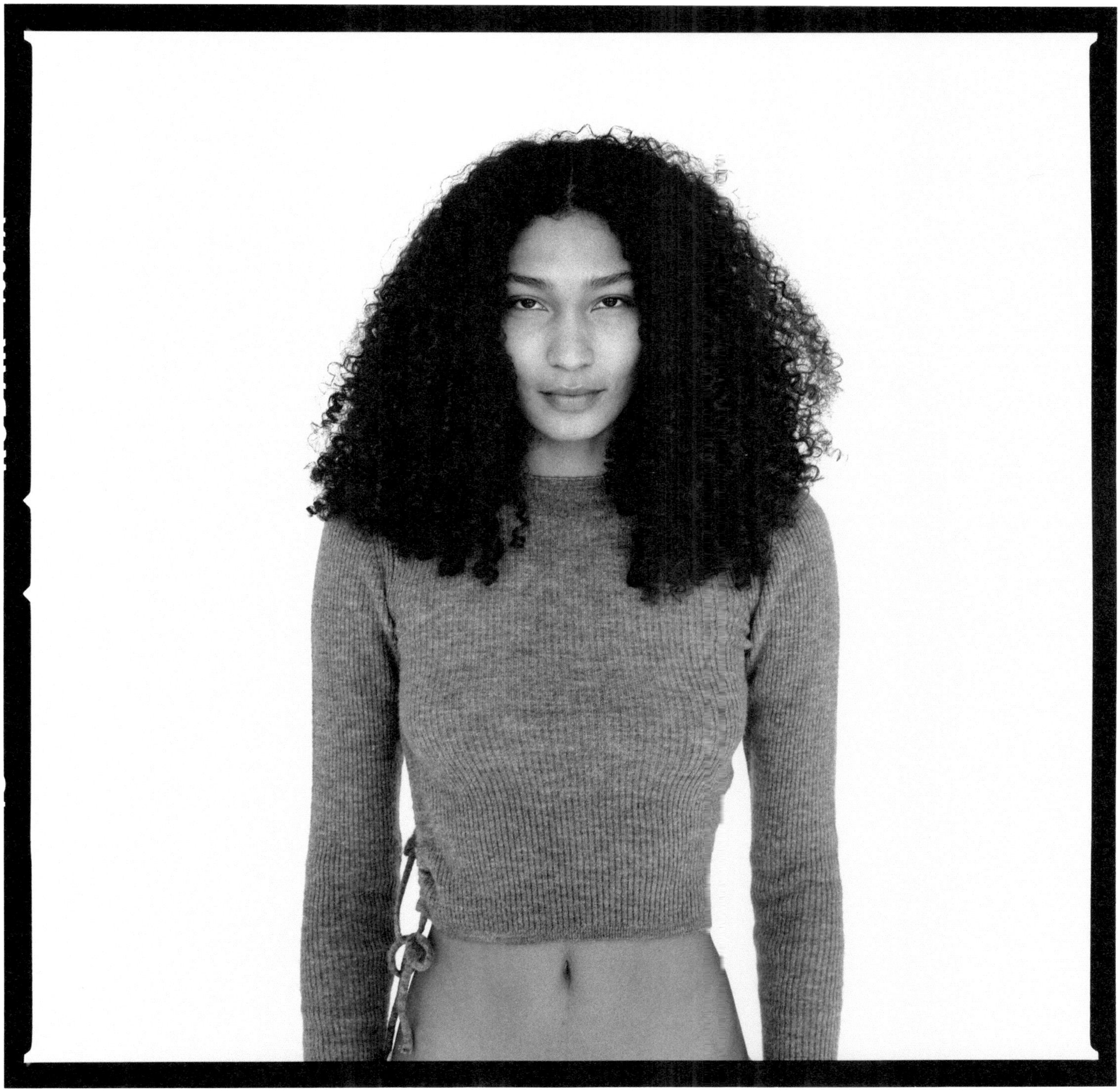

Aviana

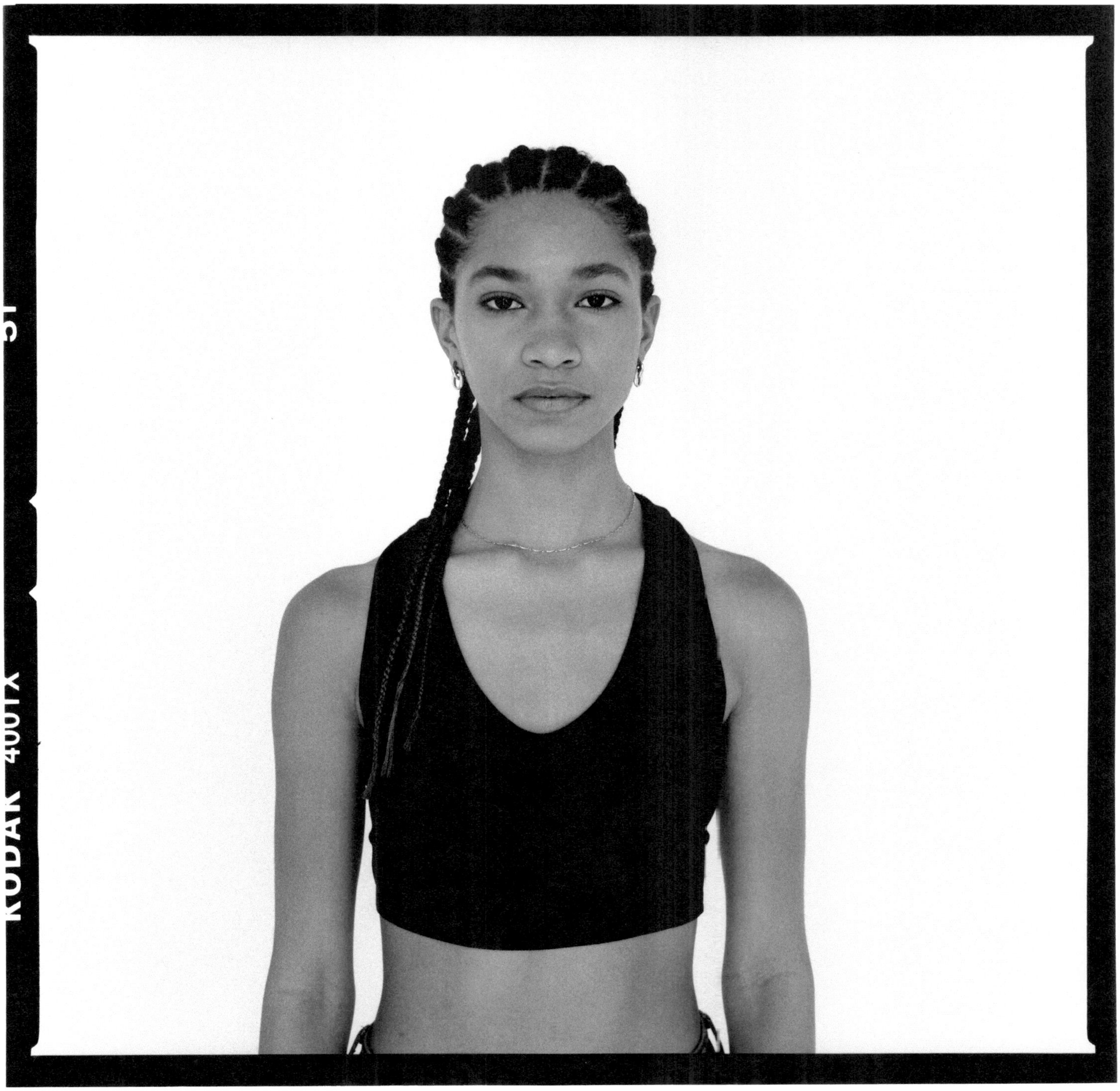
KODAK 400TX

Shreya

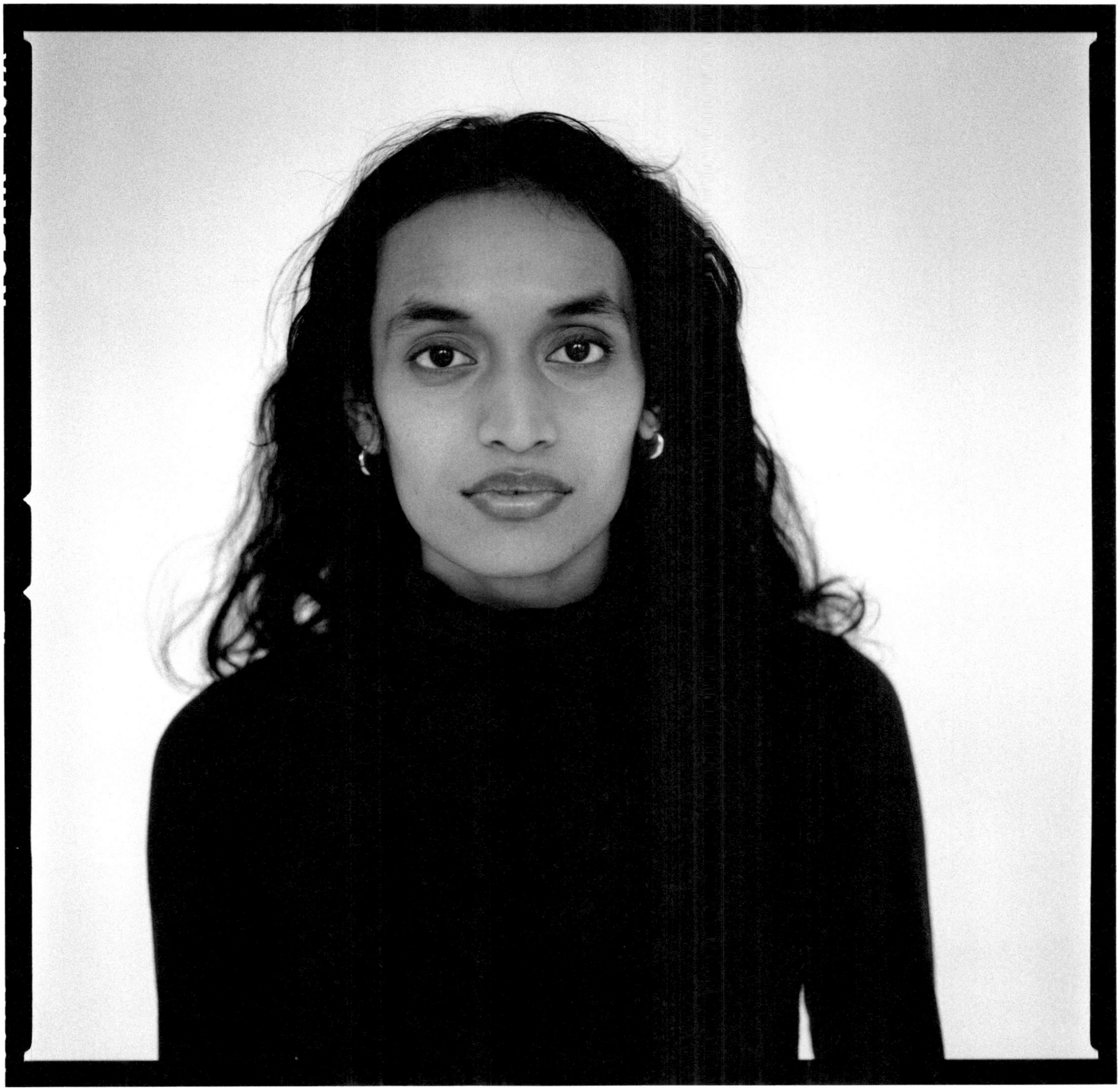

Raam

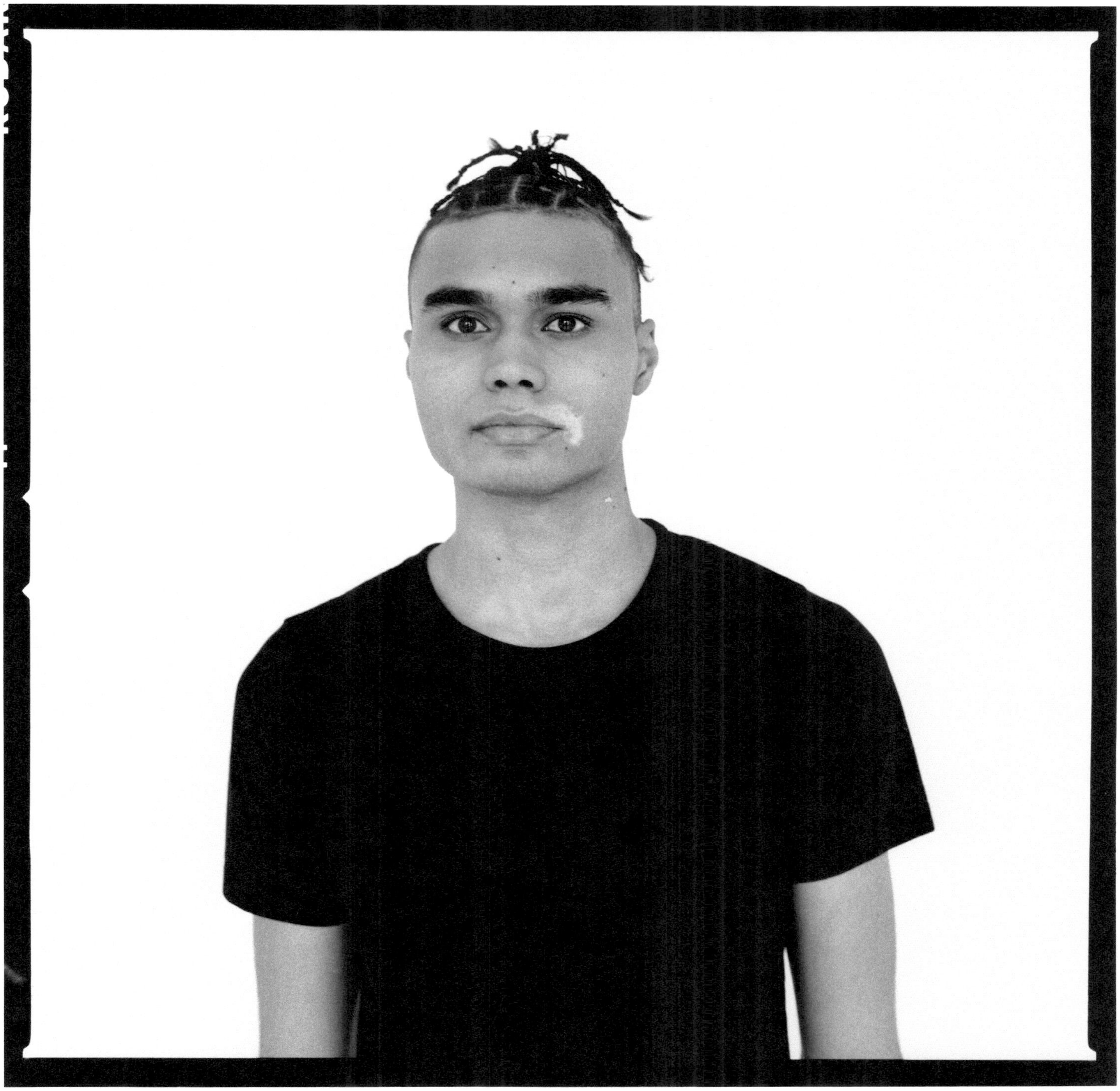

Victoria

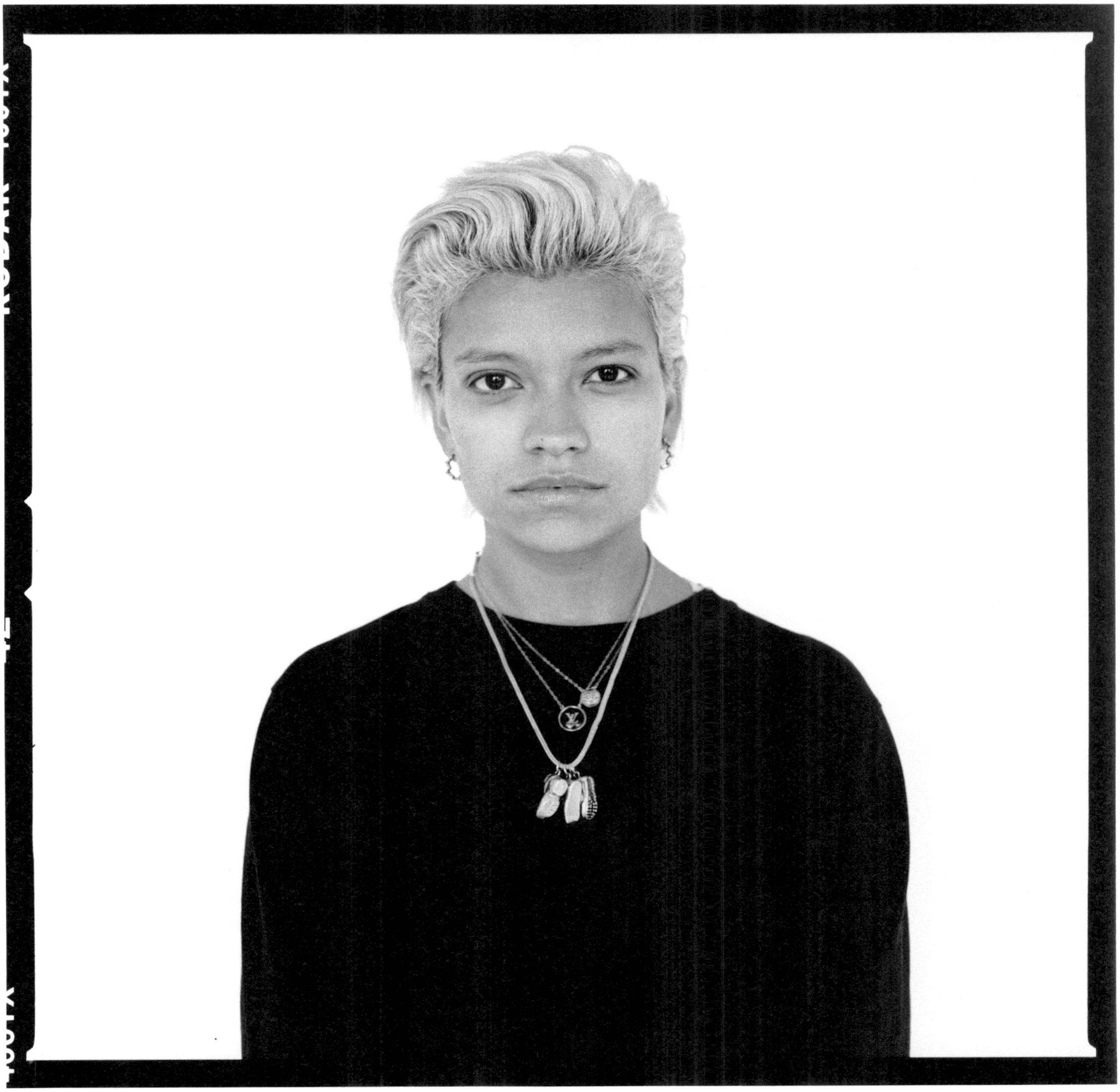

Zorka

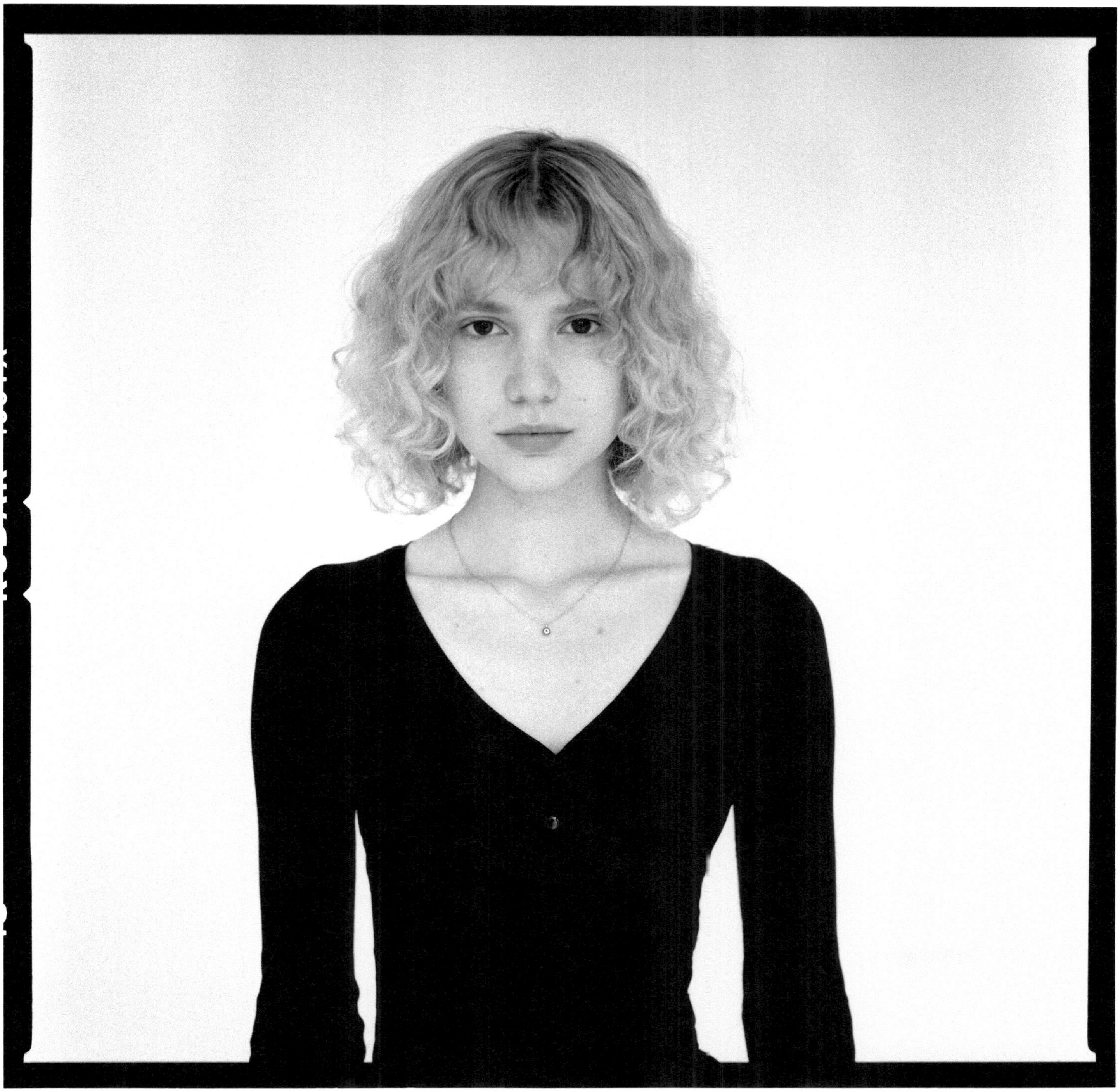

Jordan

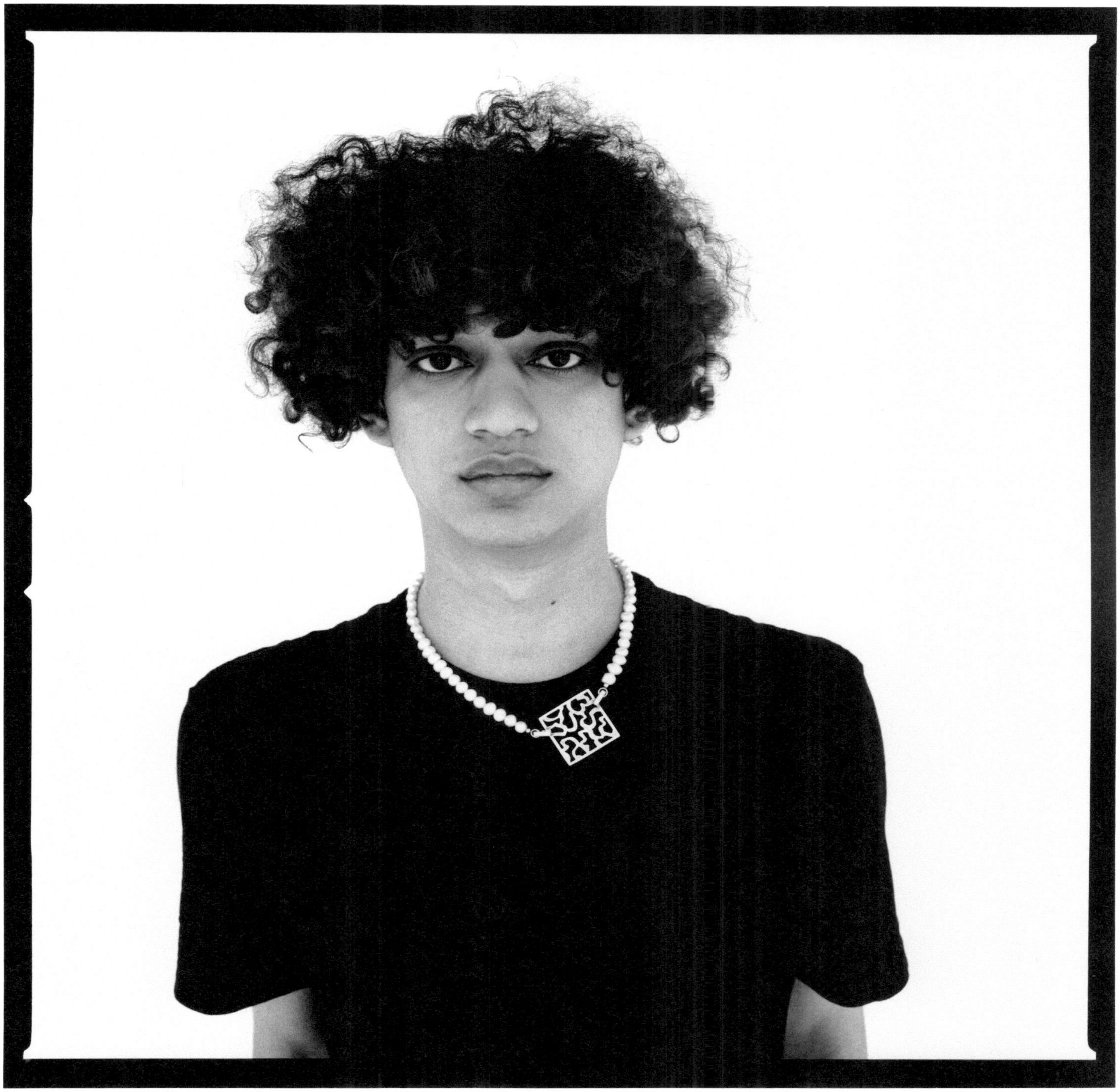

Rodrigo

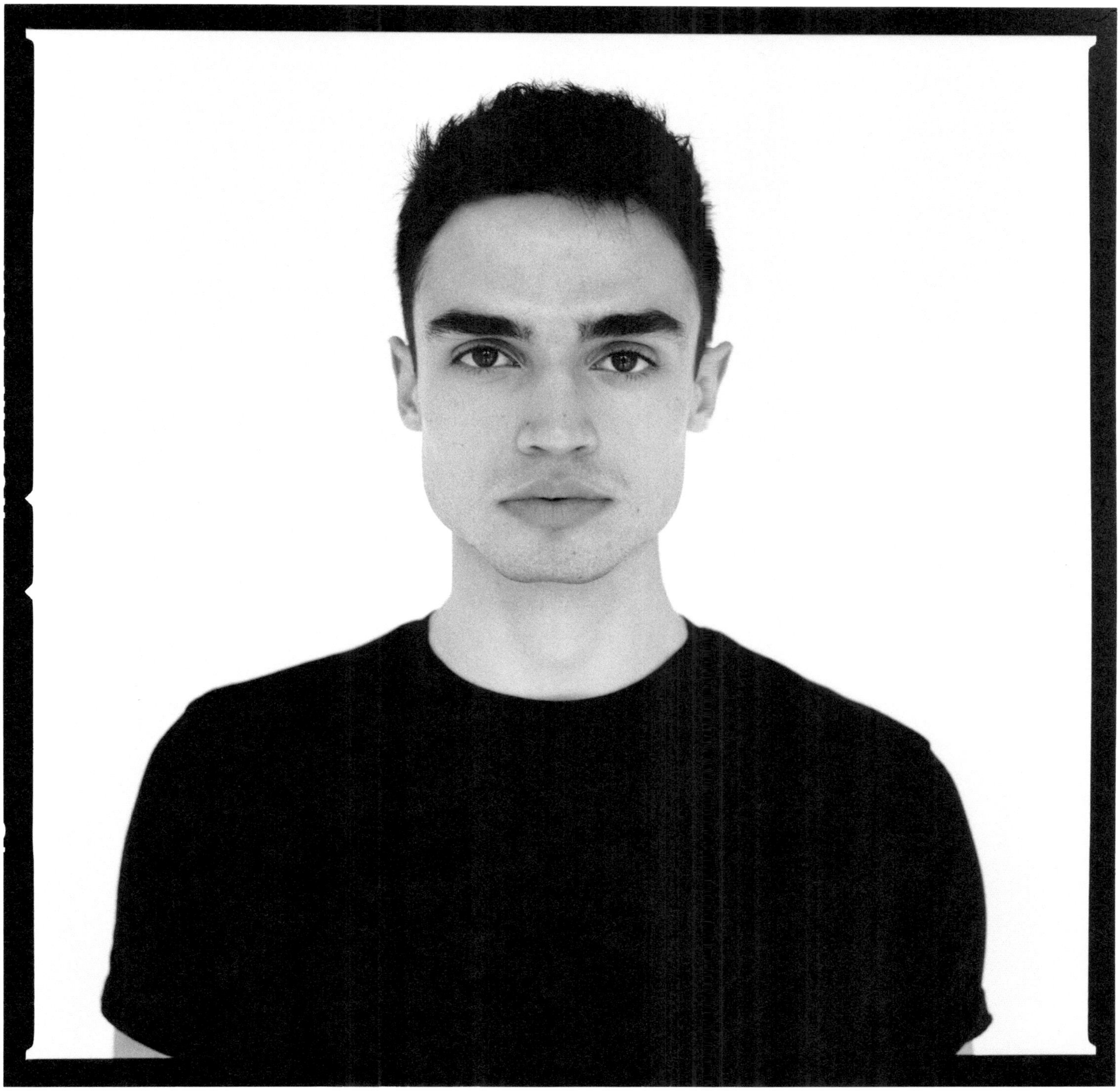

Olivia

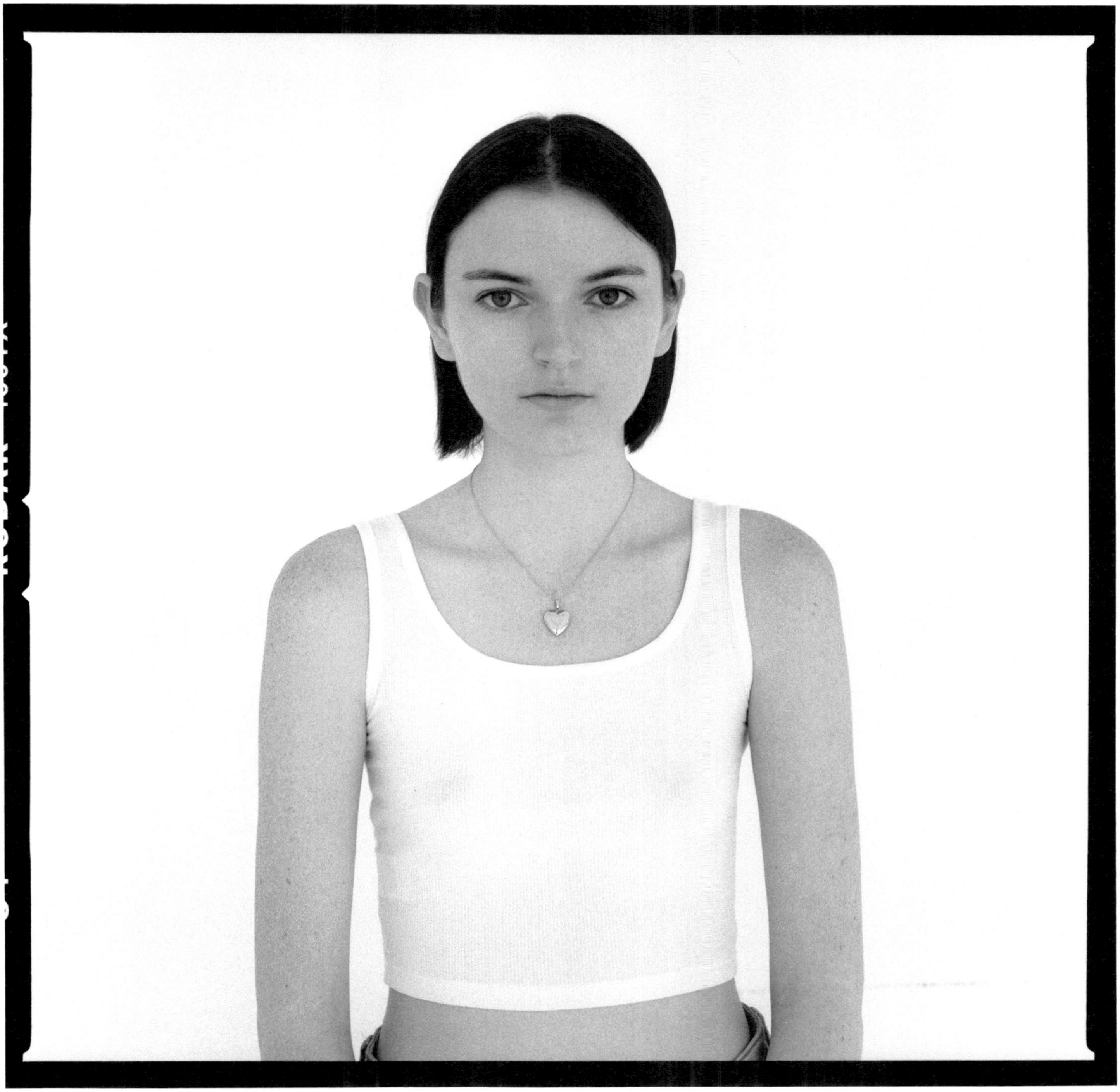

Isaiah

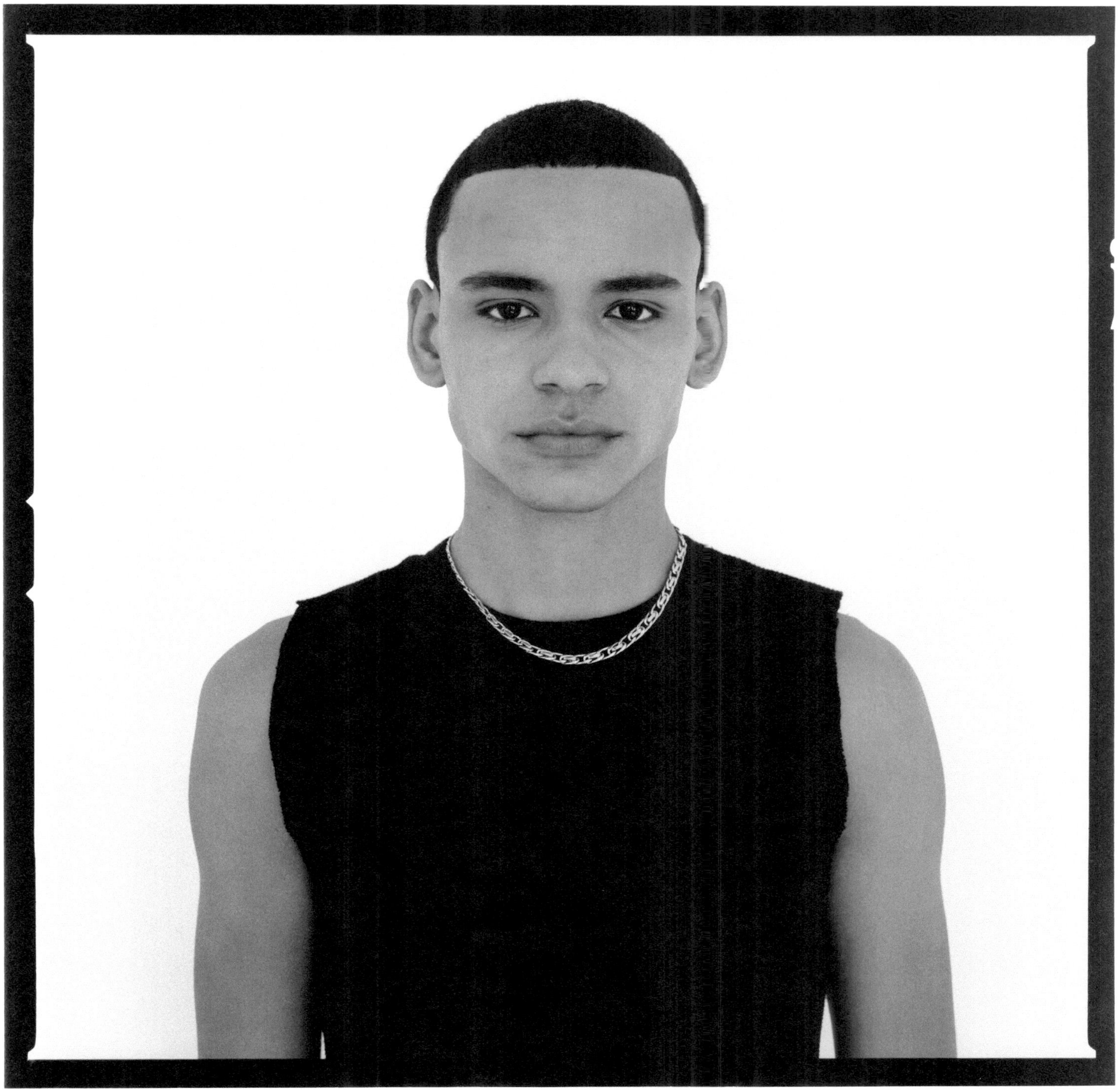

Tomie

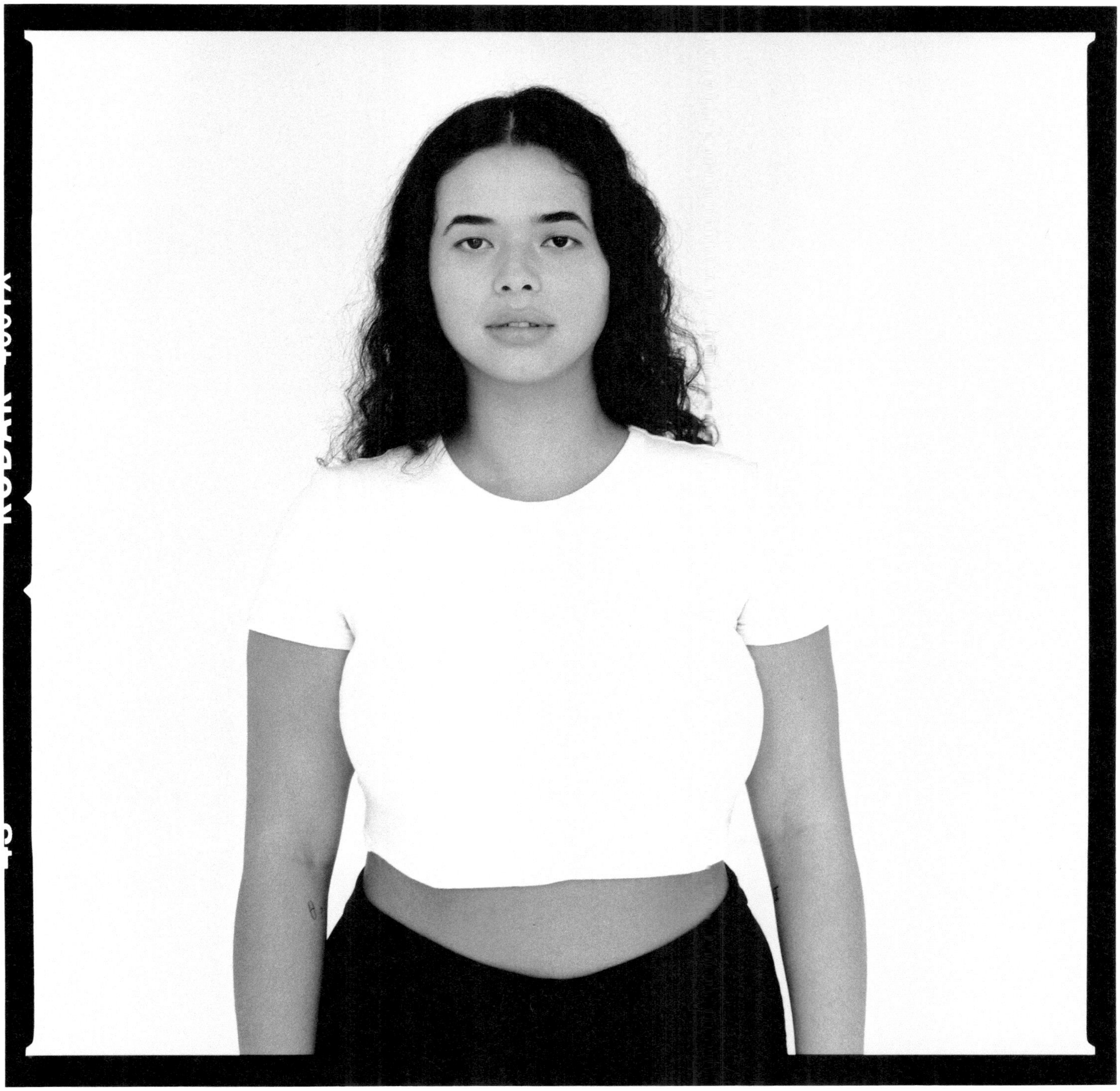

Nao/Naomi

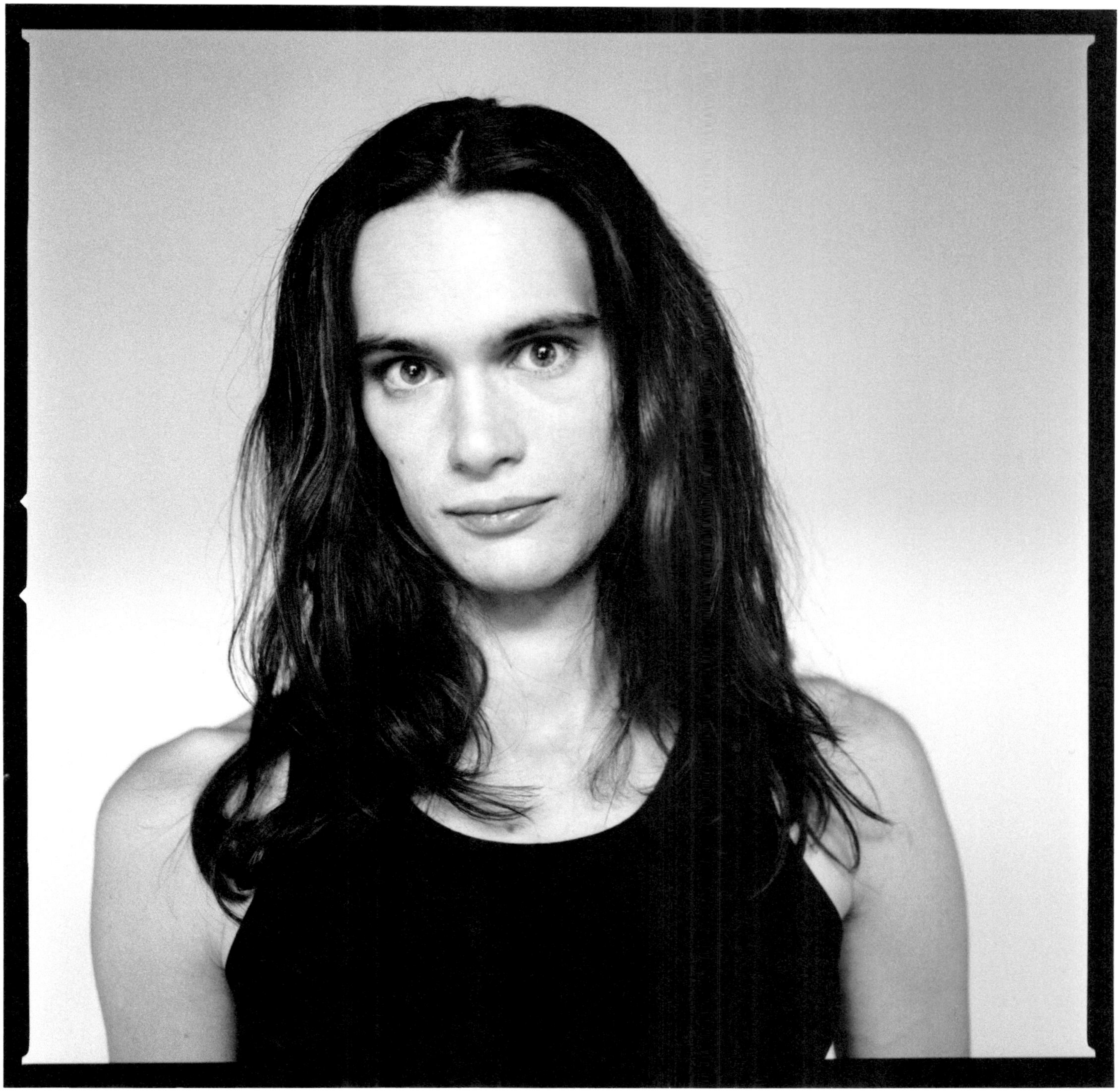

Shotaro

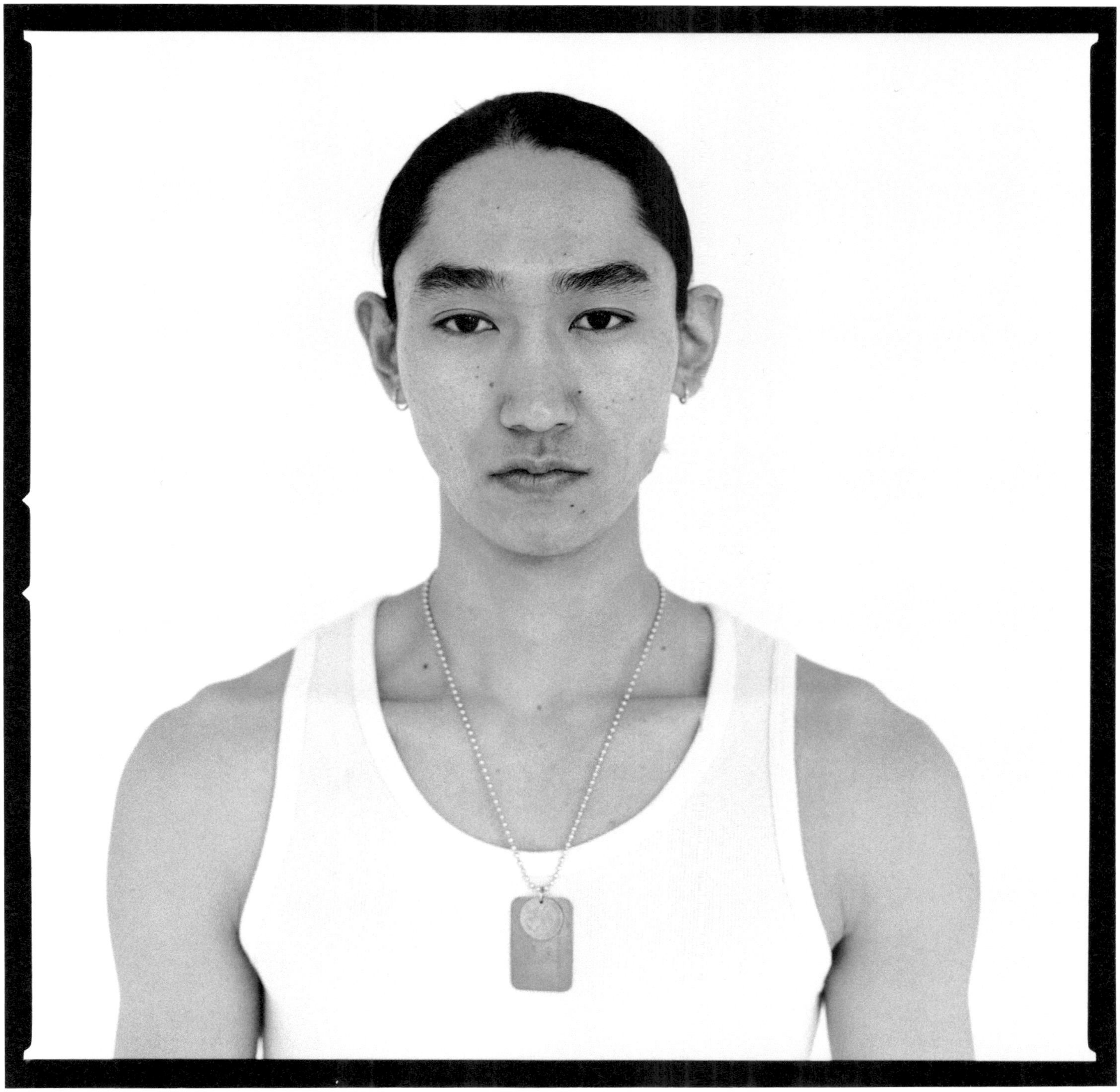

Laura

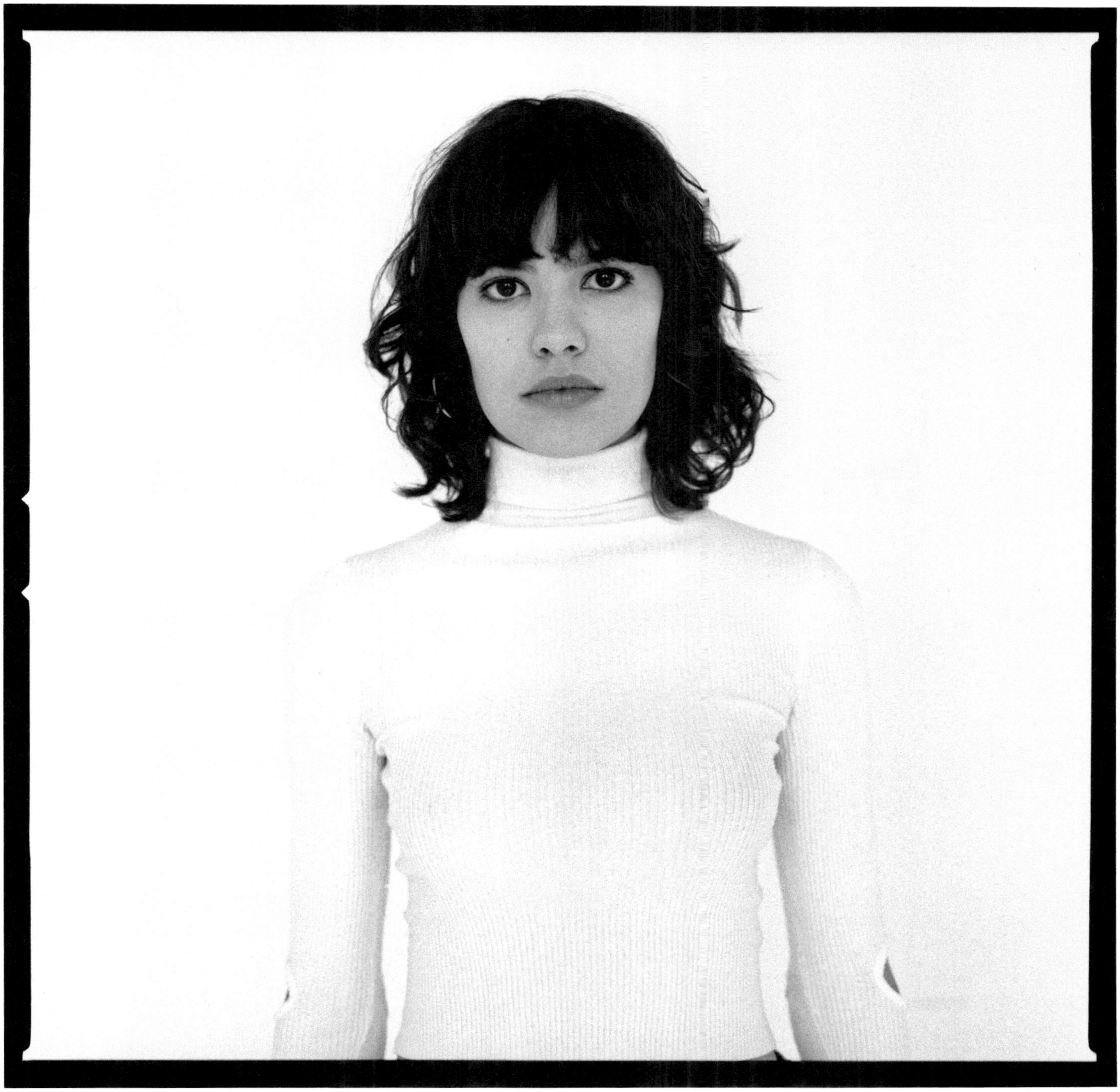

Diogo

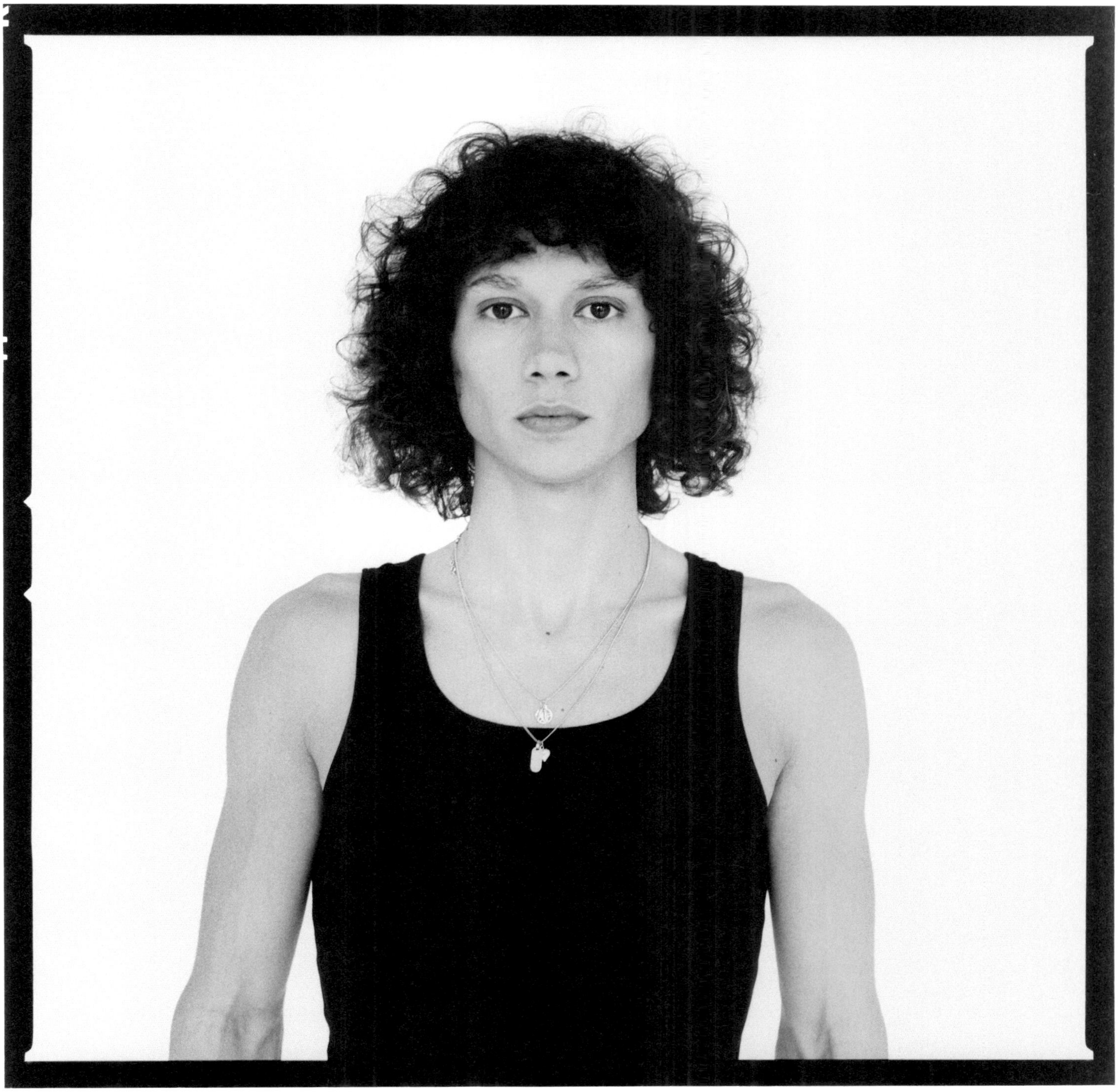

Gemma

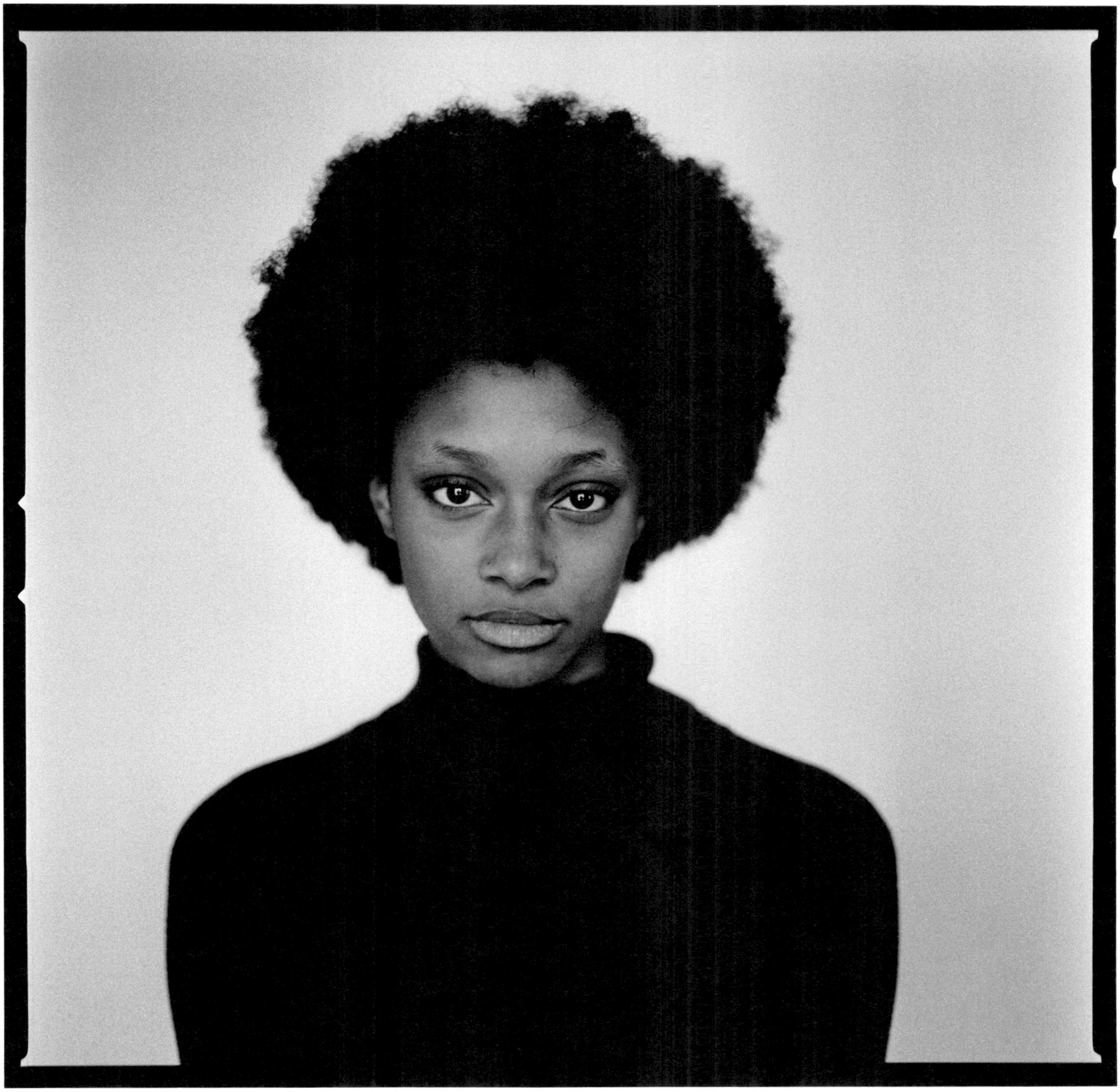

Essoye

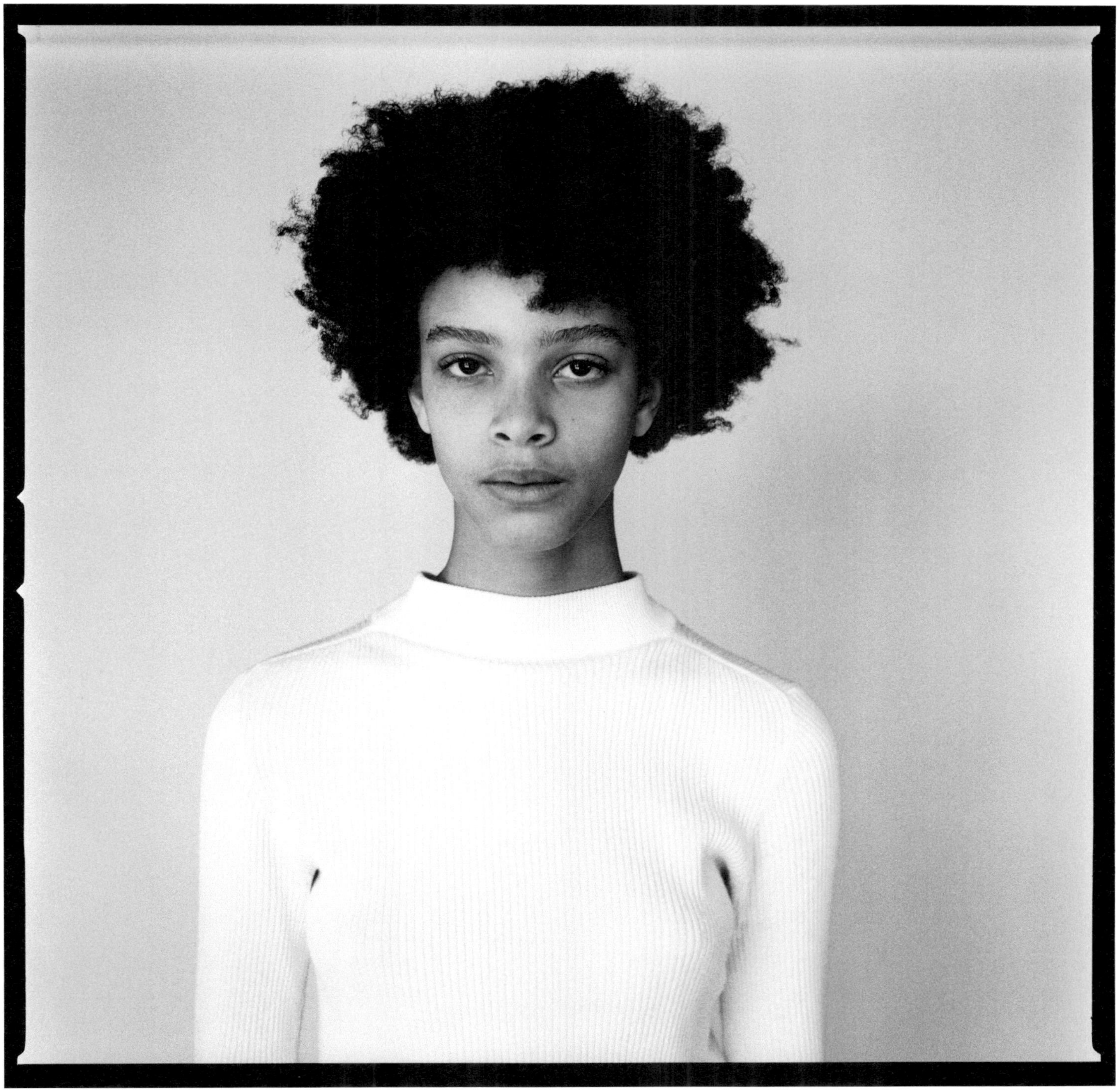

Chiara

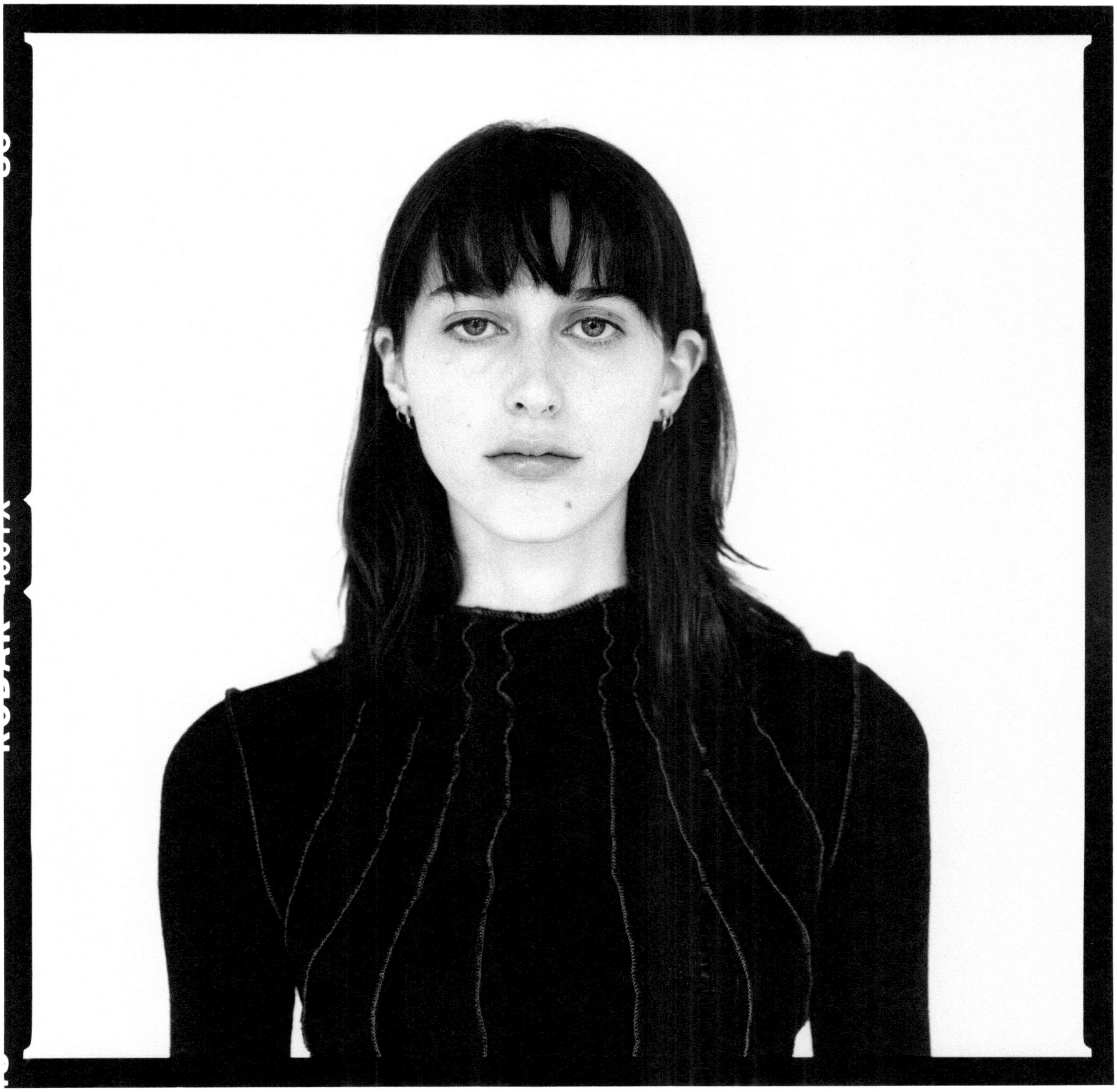

Gio

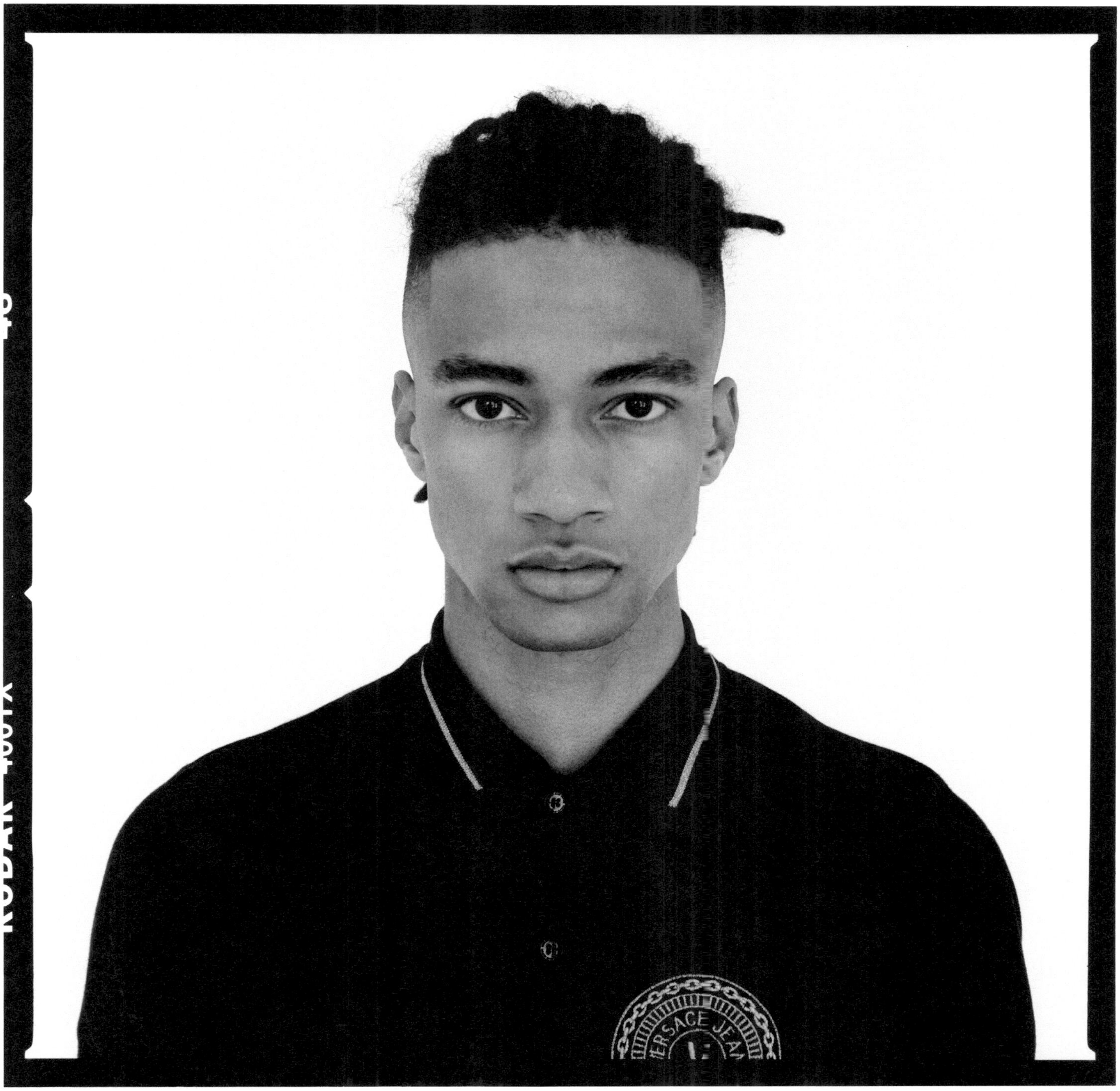

Maurana

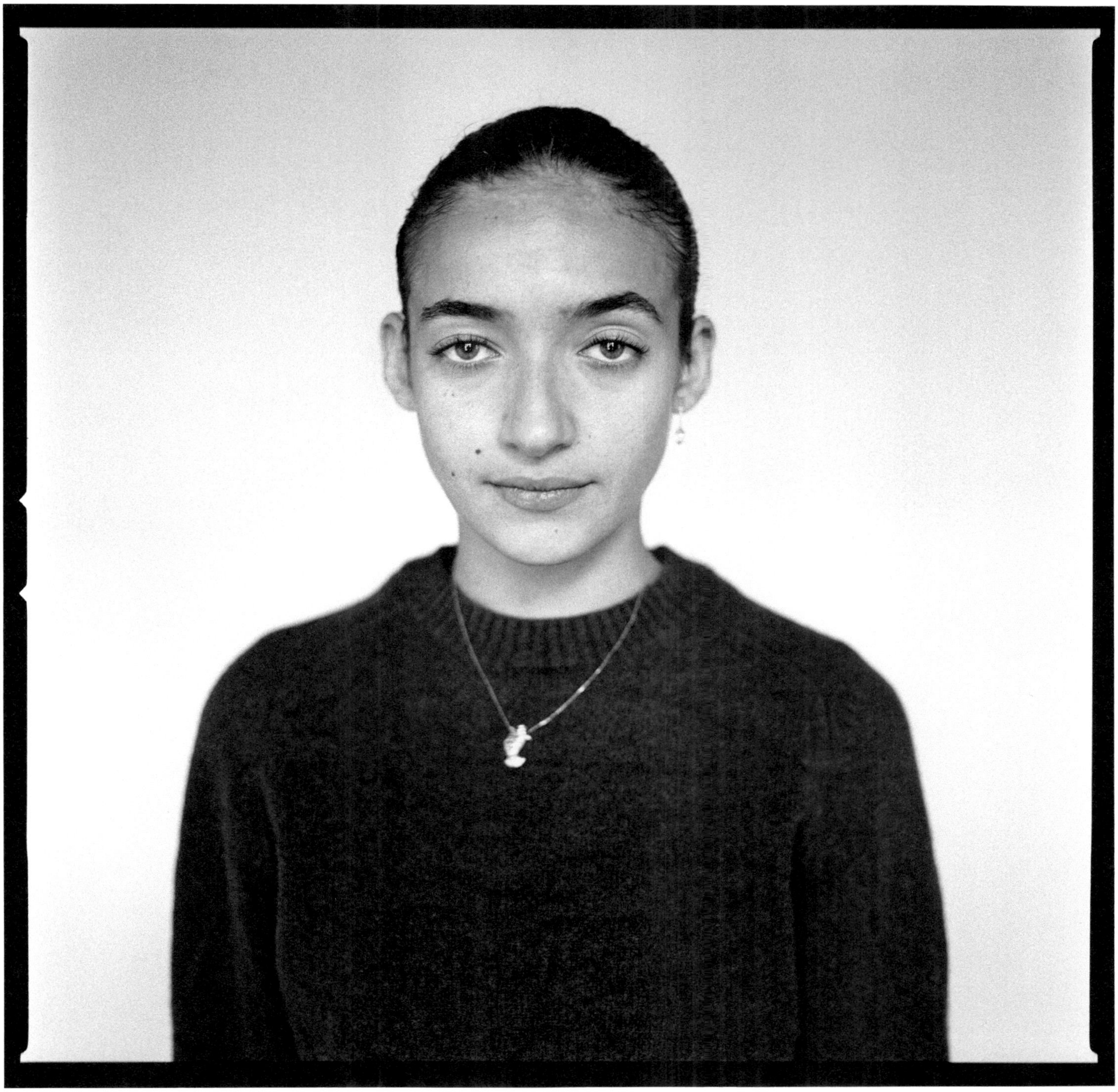

Äkyy

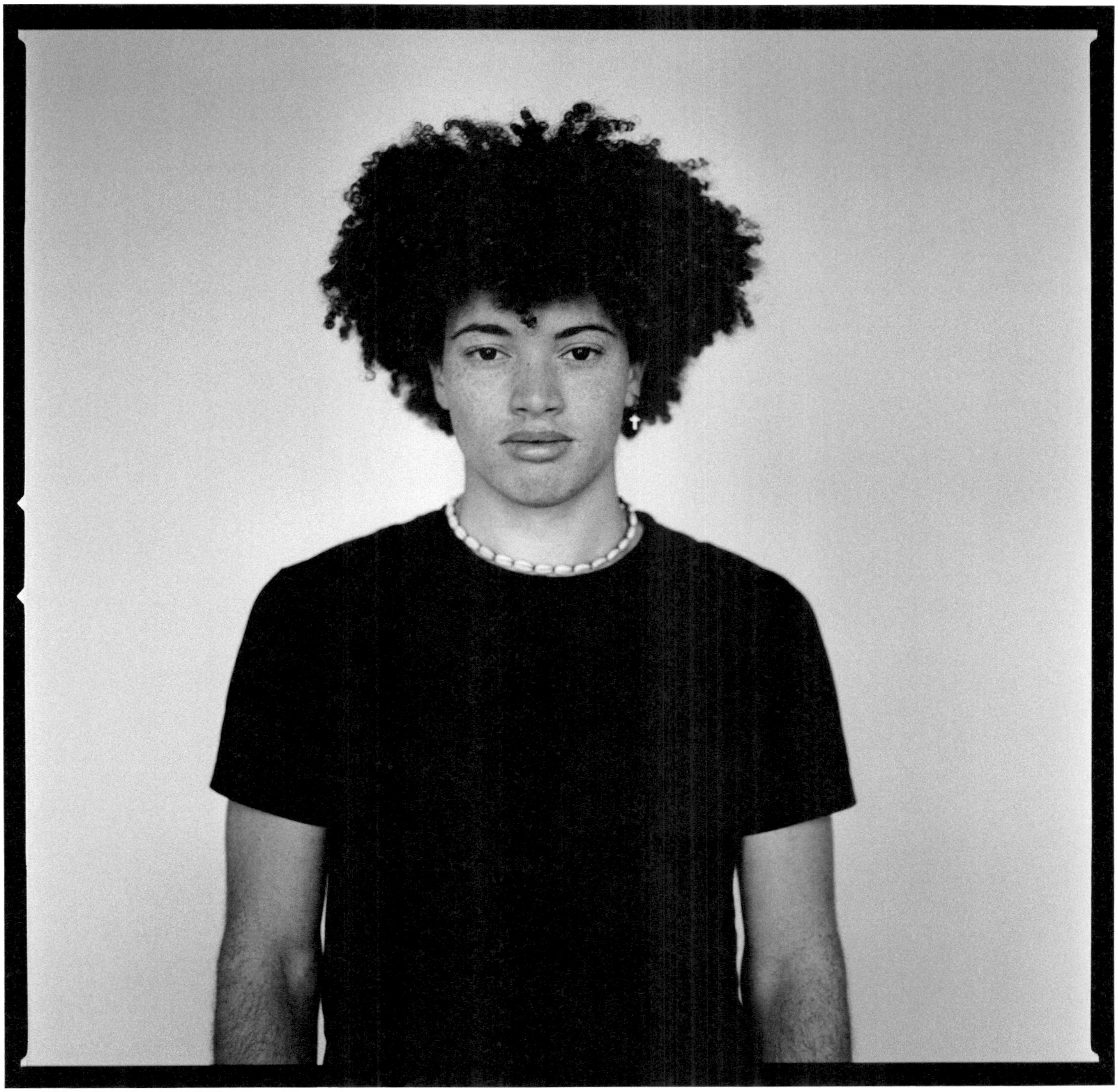

Demy

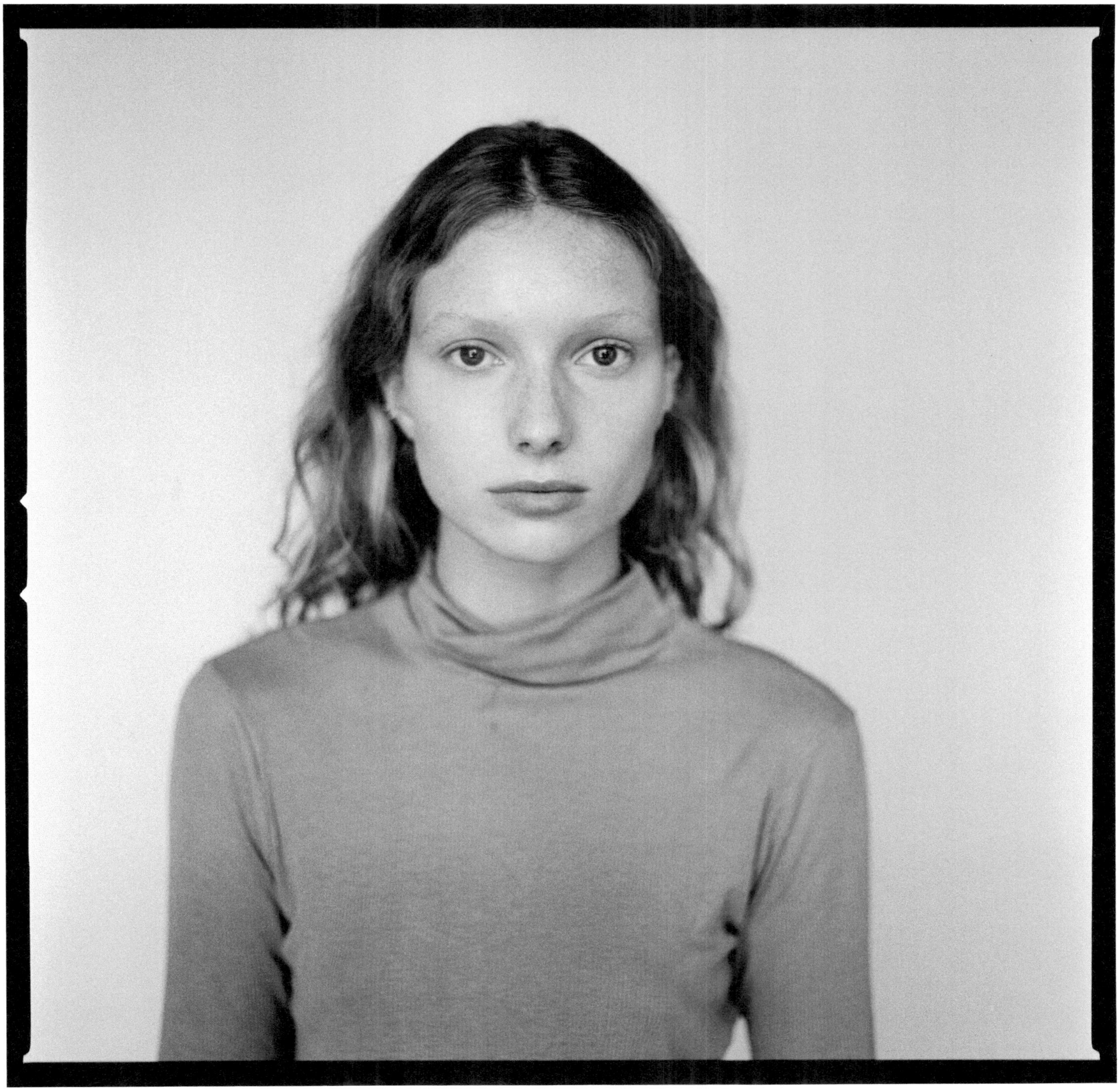

Lisa

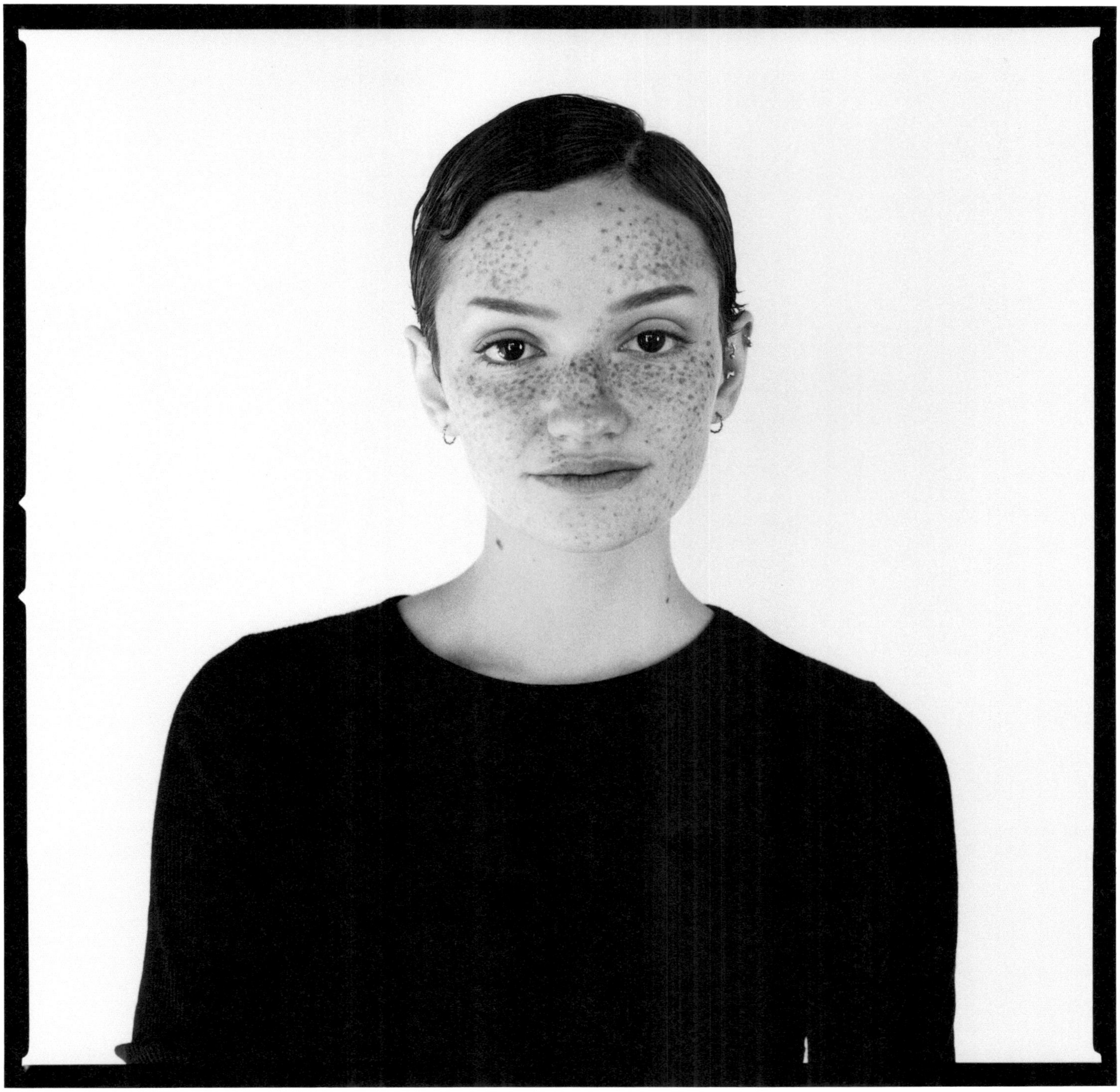

François

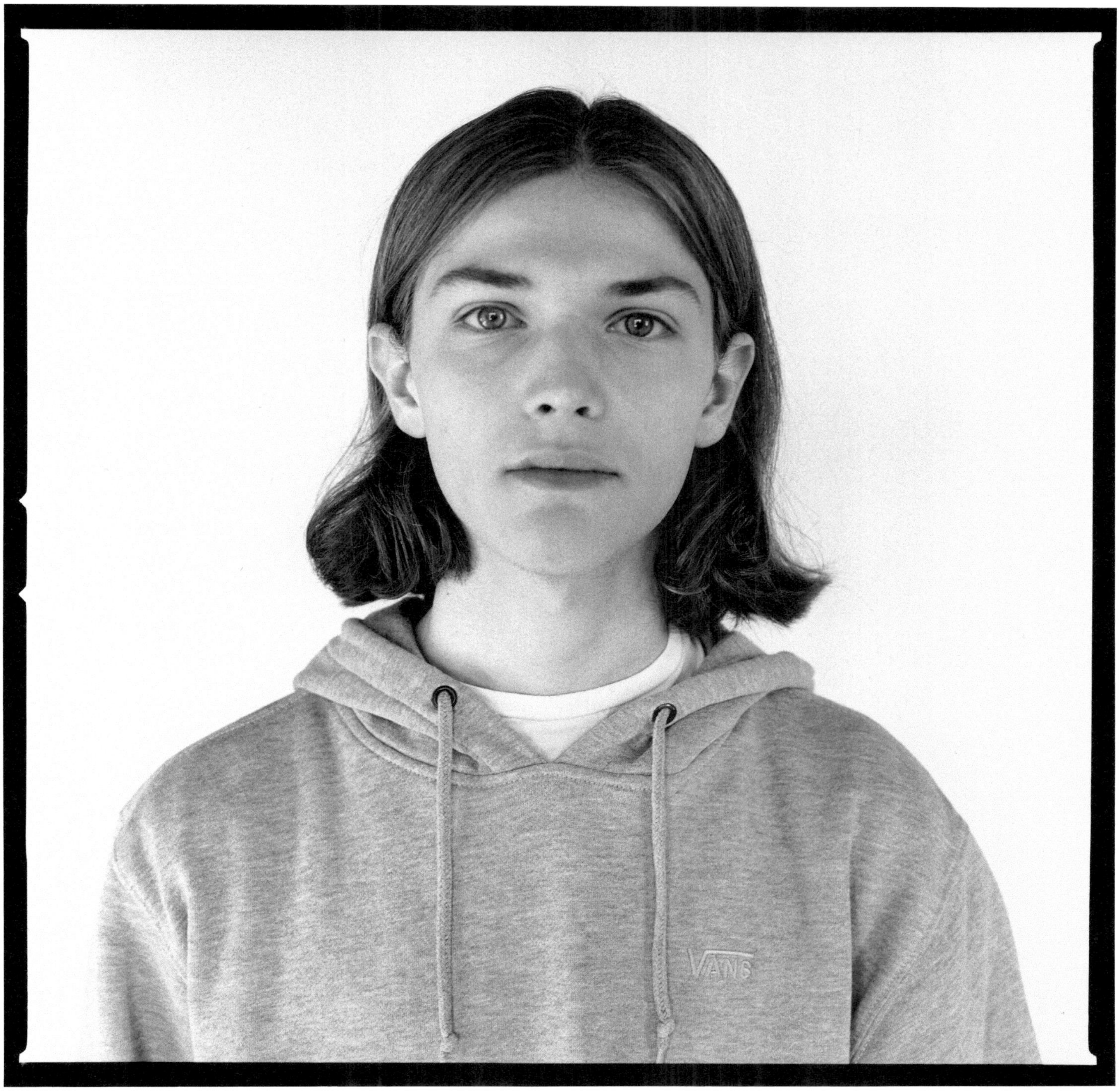
VANS

Kamy

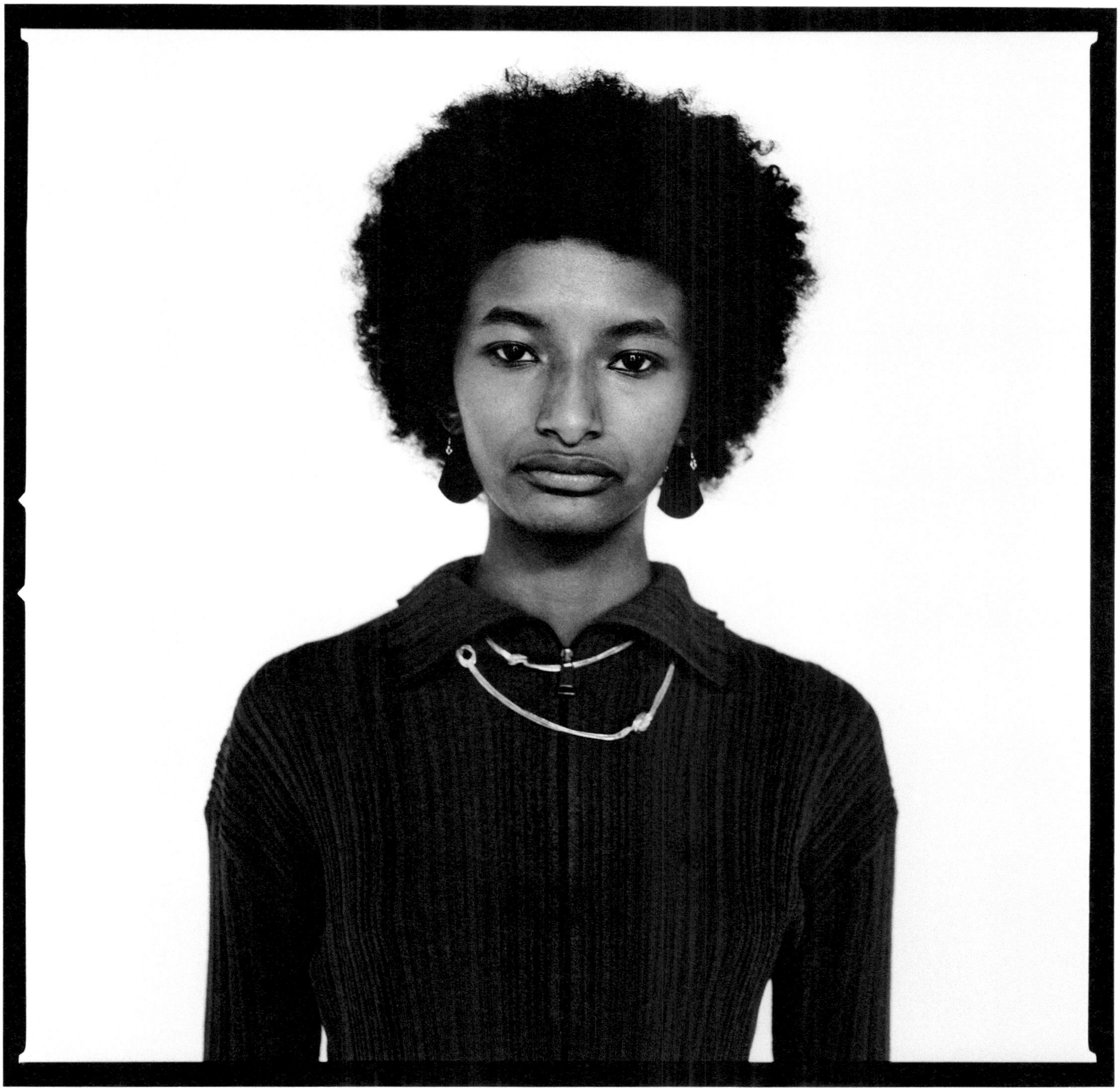

Antoine

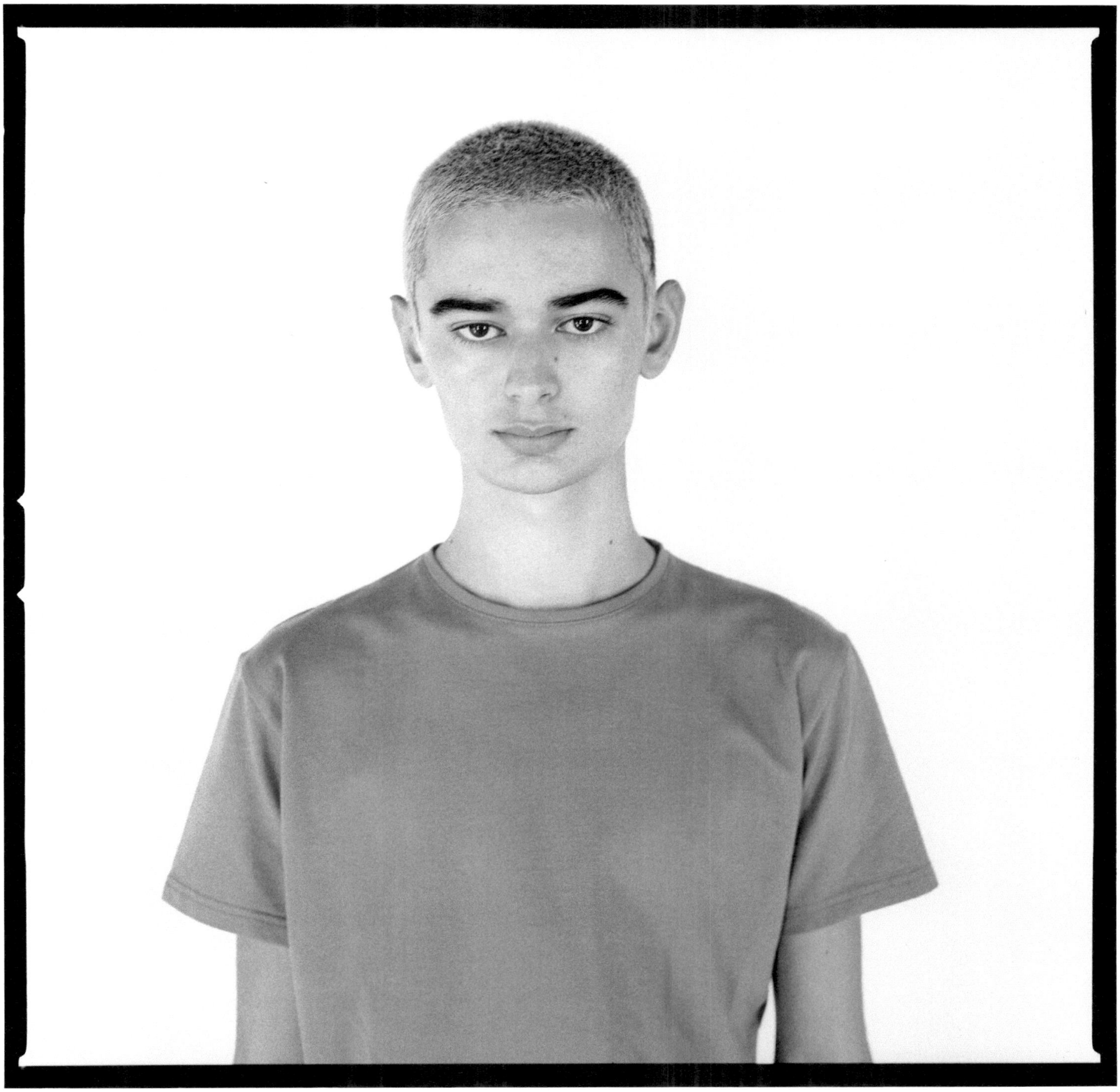

Greta

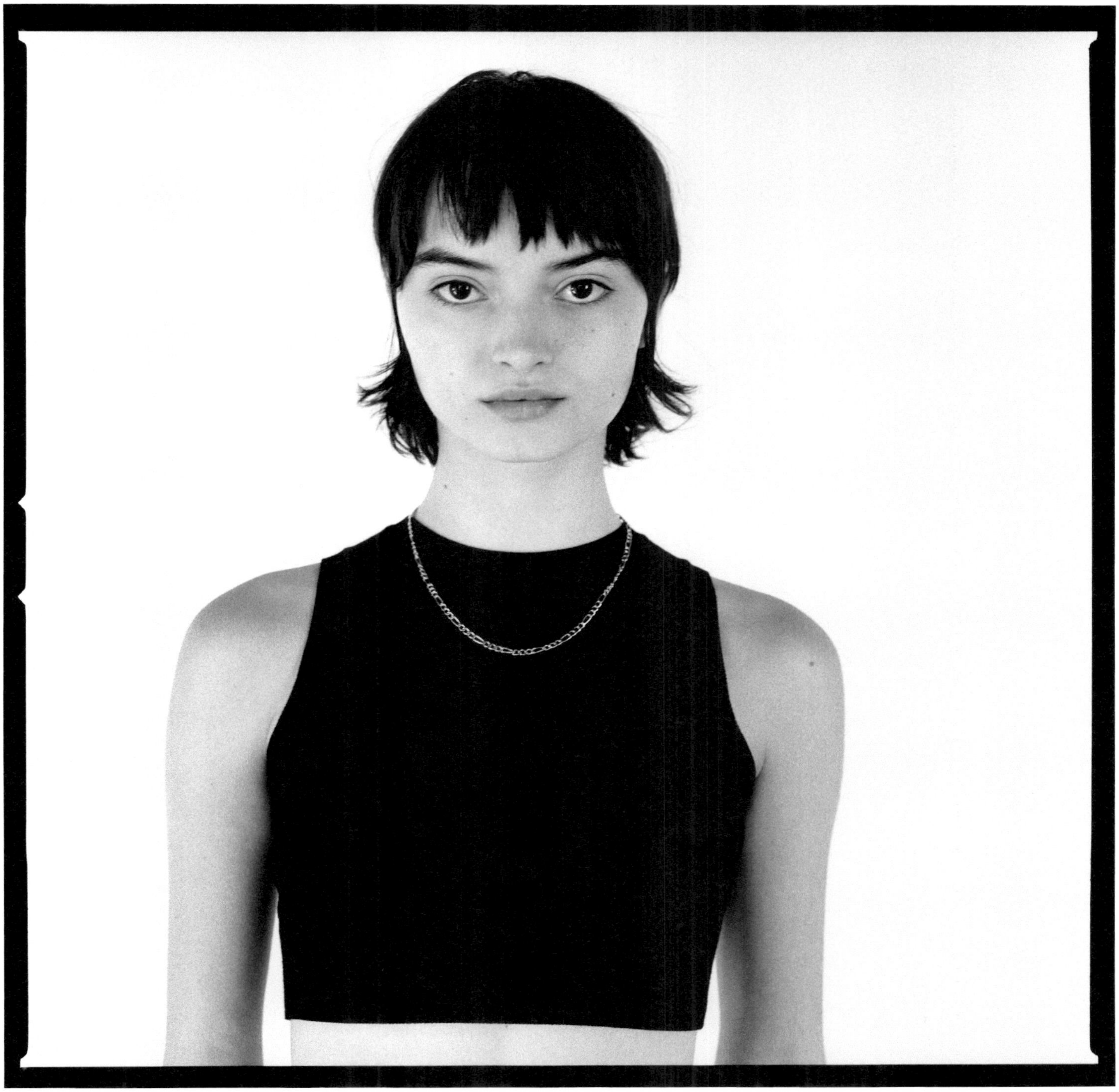

Emma

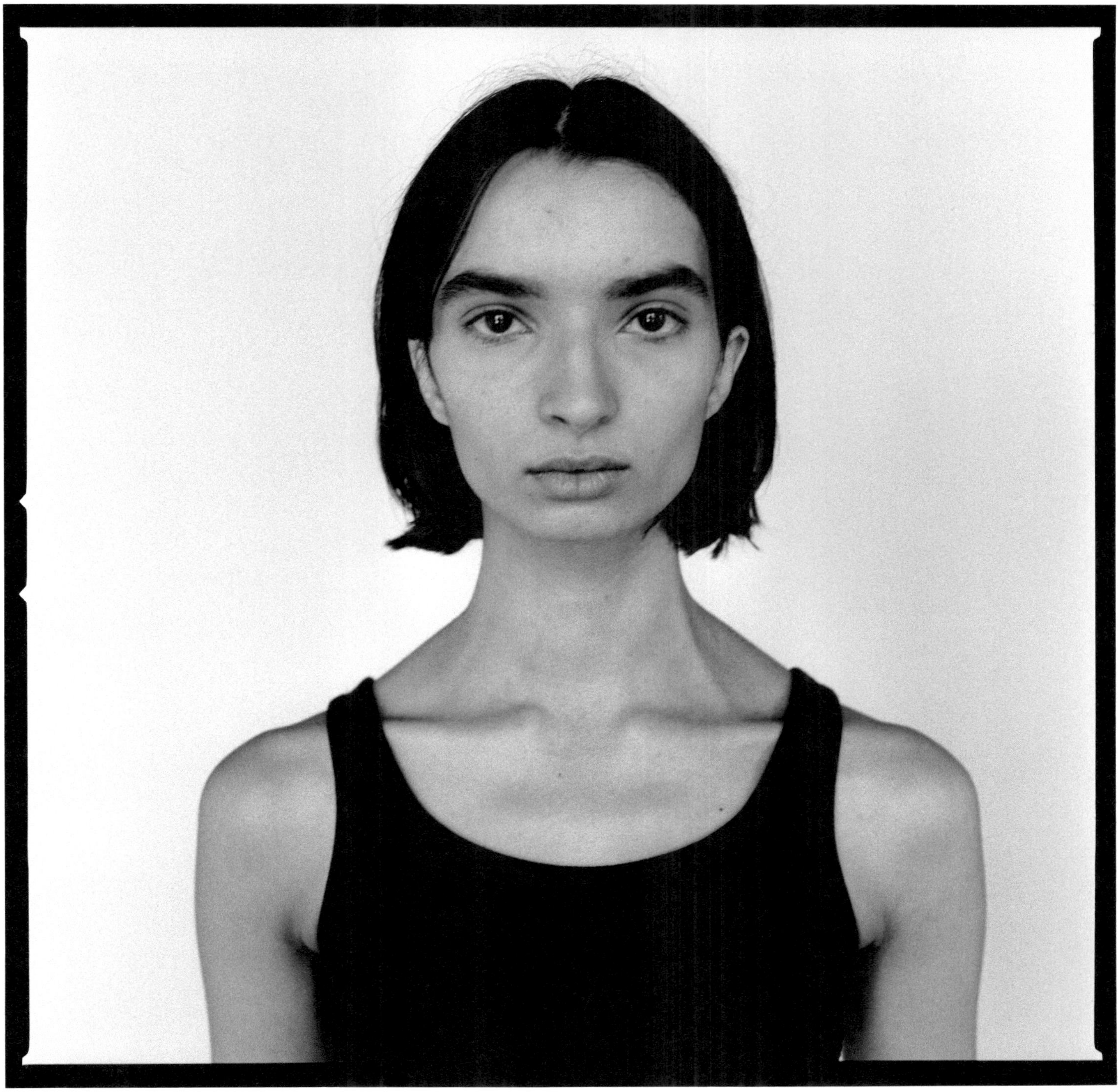

ASHKAN SAHIHI: PORTRAITS

Sussan Babaie

ParisNewYorkPortraits captures in a series of black-and-white analogue photographs a disarmingly unfiltered gaze into hopefulness. Strikingly beautiful in a way that defies standards of homogenized beauty, these faces offer a glimpse into a young urban generation that seems utterly at home in many places. Skin color, ethnic origin, national belonging, or any other category of identity politics that are so disparagingly flooding our consciousness through the political noise and media today seem unhelpful tools for learning what these young people see and want from us to see.

In these newest subjects of Ashkan Sahihi's portraits, we are invited to see something he discovered as he encountered on his return to New York—once his home—after the pandemic lockdowns of 2020–21. The return for the photographer was to a home that was the generative source of a great deal of his creativity. As in successive decades in the past, since at least the beginning of the twentieth century, in the 1980s and 1990s, when Sahihi lived and worked, and established new roots, in New York, the city was also home to a multinational, multiethnic, and multilingual community of artists, poets, philosophers, musicians, and all manner of creative aspirations. Sahihi felt at home, as so many of those people did, as I did, a fellow diasporic Iranian, in the most exciting place where we could fit right in, become new New Yorkers, albeit still alert to our being from elsewhere, or as Homi Bhabha has put it, our "in-betweenness."

Then, Sahihi and his camera roamed the city where he sought to gaze into the inner worlds of the proponents of high culture at the intersection of art and commerce in the greatest concentration, literally per square meter, of creativity and its market valuation. Never attuned to the market value of the arts—broadly defined—Sahihi's photographs of prominent artists of the period appear as a cross-section of New York's who-is-who.

Like those first series of New Yorkers, he has continued to thicken the plot with conceptual explorations of the complexities of posture of self-identity—be it by young gay men or Israeli female soldiers. And by extension, his peoples have challenged our, the viewers' own sense of personhood and belonging. The most compelling expression of that complexity of the subject and its context is the challenge he posed in his monumental series of nearly 400 photographs taken of women in Berlin. *Die Berlinerin* (2015) brings together a photographic rendition of an anthropological-social science-methodology best exemplified in Clifford Geertz's "thick description." The idea there foregrounds the enormous diversities that describe only one segment of a small corner of human society: women in just one city, Berlin. How much more might we expect from the larger spectrum of Berliners and Germans, he implicitly urges the viewer to inquire.

Where in *Die Berlinerin* we were asked to see, really encounter, the vastness of what is contained within the parameters of a single sex and city identity, in the *ParisNew YorkPortraits*, Sahihi implicates the audience through the subjects of his portraits to revisit their preconceptions in a new era. To be precise, this is the post-pandemic world where to be young and to aspire towards a bright future in such big and difficult cities as New York or Paris; those seem like impossible propositions.

Yet, these portraits, of people from New York and Paris, describe a very different world than the New Yorkers or Berliners of the past. They share one thing with every other young person from across the world: the global impact of the Coronavirus pandemic and the global lockdown that forced us all behind walls and screens but also and oddly linked us up with the whole world through new digital means of connectivity. Encountering a new post-pandemic generation of New Yorkers in his first visit back, and later of Paris, reignited his sense of fresh hope for a different future, one that is not unlike his first years of living in New York as a young emerging artist.

These are faces of young people who seem perfectly content within their skin, regardless of color or ethnic identity; we are unable to tag them with a single word: not white, or black; not Asian, African, European; maybe

Latin but also maybe from the Arabian Peninsula. That sense of comfort in one's skin comes from the confidence that the mixed-race, multi-ethnic children of the past see as the norm in the future. This is not comforting in an age of anti-everything-that-is-not "pure"! Sahihi speaks of his new subjects as not only filled with youthful energy and hopeful spirit of the possibilities laid ahead, but more touchingly of the ways in which they see themselves as the future of humanity.

That none of them can easily be pigeonholed—none is "purely" of one or another race, ethnicity or of other markers of single identity—is captured in Sahihi's personal conversations with his subjects: they possess singularly easy ways to fit into their skin. That condition reminds Sahihi of his own children; and me of mine! This new generation of urban youth, some indeed identifying with a particular ancestry, seem to have emerged in the post-pandemic life across the greatly diverse populations with an awareness of their most distinctive asset: their global connectivity, and its possibilities. It may seem foolhardy to speak of such aspirations for the future at a time when in parts of the world the sentiment against the "other" is articulated in terms of impurity and has become dark and dangerous. Yet, Sahihi sees through his lens, as does anyone who encounters the youth on a regular basis, the hopeful signs of a future in which few can ever claim purity of race or ethnicity while at the same time they may in fact be celebrating the confidence and almost timeless hopefulness that is surprising for our present condition. These portraits remind us, as Sahihi aims to do, of the fact that these youthful subjects retain a sense of individuality rooted in being from and belonging to more than one place.

TO BE LOOKED AT AND TO BE SEEN

Saskia Trebing

To be looked at and to be seen are two very different things. In our digital age of constant exposure to images (an ungraspable approximate of 100 million photographs and videos are uploaded to Instagram every day) one could argue that for many people to be looked at is the norm—but really to be seen is actually rare.

As we speak, during the last days of a dizzying 2025, humans have been in front of cameras for more than one and a half centuries. But this does not mean there is a playbook for the delicate act of turning somebody into an image. Every generation has to recalibrate their relation to photography. Even though it's been done—and written about—countless times before, every encounter between photographer and the photographed is unique and an irreplaceable particle in the conglomerate we call art history.

For his recent portrait series *ParisNewYorkPortraits* photographer Ashkan Sahihi has chosen a time-honored way of taking pictures: with medium-format analogue camera, black-and-white, natural light, monochrome white to grayish background. Every one of the young protagonists (the age range is eighteen to twenty-eight) looks right at the spectator. The title puts a little buzz in your head; involuntarily, you are looking for discreet visual signs of the French capital and the American metropolis—both of them cities that carry an inescapable legacy in the history of photography and a vague promise of cosmopolitism. Is this title the easiest way to dress these human beings in an aura of interestingness and feed on the myths we have tied to these places? Is there something French in the face of this woman? Does this guy carry his (real or fake?) black Versace polo shirt through the streets of Bushwick or Belleville? But this approach turns out to be a trap. There's nothing to gain from these detective-like questions, except proof for the persistent—and limiting—urge to place someone.

Portraits have always been a means of communication, but with the arrival of camera-phones and social media the function of these images has fundamentally changed. As writer Nathan Jurgenson already argued in 2019,[1] most images do not compete with the traditional notion of photography any longer. Rather, they are units of communication that are tied to a specific context, platform, and audience.

The people appearing in Ashkan Sahihi's series have grown up in a world of unprecedented potential visibility. Whereas young adulthood is by definition a time of self-creation and making an image of who you want to be, that process is turned into a public spectacle that can be watched (or rather consumed) globally. The promise is supposed to be in the messy amalgam of algorithmic preferences, platform capitalism, and instant diffusion of trends. Everyone can be a brand. Attention is an economic value, and to hold the gaze of the ever-scrolling audience for just a few seconds is the most you can hope for.

One can safely assume that the majority of Sahihi's opposites/counterparts in *ParisNewYorkPortraits* are used to sharing photos of themselves online. To be effective, these images have to be "readable." Algorithms love predictability – not really surprising as they are especially good at pattern recognition. One could say that their "need" to place someone in fixed categories is just as pronounced as the human equivalent, maybe even more so.

To find a context that you want to be defining for yourself can be liberating—and the chance to find solidarity and appreciation for nonconforming identities in online communities is still a great relief for many. But to make yourself visible comes with a price. Not only have portraits become a vessel for constant judgment and comparison; the machinery of social media also forces everybody who gets into this game to think about images of themselves strategically. The questions that fit an individual into a grid—Who are they? What are they?—need to be answered to become a reliable brand. The alleged freedom to become whatever you want can come with the loss of the freedom to be ambiguous or many things at once.

This tendency also has an effect on the perception of artistic photography. As Ashkan Sahihi recalls of his shootings

in Paris and New York, one question was asked by many of the protagonists when they entered the studio: What should I do? This inquiry might be understood as an internalized expectation—I'm supposed to match an idea that someone else has of me. That notion is shaken when the answer is "nothing."

To simply trust a situation and allow a loss of control over how you are seen is one of the big adventures that comes with art. Of course, these portraits are talking to the viewer as much as any image floating around. But what they are saying is anything but obvious.

The photos in Sahihi's series show how different that "nothing" can look in faces and bodies. Some of the sitters seem to be challenging the camera, others look kind of questioning. None of them turn their gaze away. They are definitely seeing us, but are we really seeing them?

As all of these 38 people are brought together in an exhibition and a book, it seems natural to ask, what do they have in common. We don't know much more than their first names, their approximate age range, and that they either live in Paris or New York. We can assume that some of their formative experiences (growing into a digital cosmos of images, being potentially connected to anyone on this planet, experiencing racism, facing a future of aggravated climate crisis, and the rise of far-right politics) are similar on both sides of the Atlantic.

But is that really enough to imagine them as any kind of collective? A generation even? Or is this urge to make meaning of this selection some kind of displacement activity because it has become so challenging to just accept an image as a "secret about a secret," as Diane Arbus put it more than fifty years ago? The mostly plain clothes on the "chosen ones," the discreet makeup and accessories, the consistent framing and the unitizing background of the studio makes it impossible to read these people as ambassadors for something, let alone a brand.

The composition of images in this project is first and foremost the decision of an artist—maybe the opposite of an algorithmic hierarchy. Pointing the camera at these individuals can mean a recognition or an imposition—as portrait photography always has. There is a lot of things we don't know about these protagonists presented to us, but we know that their photographic effigy is the result of a specific pact between photographer and model in the studio; a place that may be physically placed in Paris or New York, but which at the same time is extracted from these cities and becomes its own realm.

Identity is not questioned here: the existence of different phenotypes, genders, and ethnic backgrounds is a fact, but not "the topic" of this series. And maybe that is the biggest difference compared to the presumed lived experience of these young adults. They're constantly confronted with the demand to explain and define themselves – both aesthetically and politically. Social media requires a legible curated image that can be sold; and the systemic racisms in both Europe and the United States leads to an environment in which their existence has to be defended.

None of this can be ignored regarding *ParisNewYorkPortraits*. But at the same time these portraits are a chance to look at these faces without the instant necessity for "answers." They are here. They exist. Not to be read. But to be seen.

1 Nathan Jurgenson, *The Social Photo: On Photography and Social Media* (New York: Verso, 2019).

NEW YORK/PARIS
EXAMINING THE FACE

Natascha Schoenaich-Carolath

The center of gravity in Ashkan Sahihi's photography, its organizing principle, is the human face. In New York in the 1980s and 1990s, he took portraits of creatives and artists. Their faces were already, or would soon become, icons of literature, the fine arts, and hip-hop. In his first conceptual series, a pair of white-gloved hands manipulates the flesh of the faces of eighteen models. Its title is *Faces*. In the series that follow, Sahihi goes on to explore the appearance of the human face in the borderlands of identity, the interstices between expression and experience.

In the *Drug* Series, his subject is the faces of intoxicated people, taken in an almost clinical studio set-up. The pictures document the facial movements on a full dose of crack, cocaine, mescaline, and other drugs, with only the photographer present, the participant, a companion of their choosing, and a nurse. In a similarly reduced setup, Sahihi examines the faces of people hypnotized into different emotional states. This time, it is the hypnotist's words and the participant's imagination that shape the facial expressions. While other series explore the face in wider, more sociological contexts, like that of young female IDF soldiers or Berlin working women, his *Mirror* Series also possesses a concentrated focus on the face in a minimalist studio setting. Portraits of people, alone in a small, prepped box, looking at their own face for twenty minutes, and photographed from behind a one-way mirror.

Even in their absence, they play a prominent role. Not long after the release of the Guantanamo Bay files and the ensuing scandal around the torture of prisoners and the detainment of innocent people, Sahihi got the opportunity to photograph Camp X-Ray. Despite all efforts to get the permit to photograph the inmates, all of the pictures taken show a ghostly architecture void of humans. Their invisibility speaks of the unspeakable nature of their experience of the psychological, sexual, and physical violence they were exposed to.

A Class in Jewish-Persian Morphology

It was this preoccupation with and curiosity about the face that led Sahihi to take a course in human morphology with psychoanalyst Dr. Catherine Shainberg. Attendants would explore "the significance behind body forms and shapes, and how these attributes resonate through mythological archetypes." The field of psychology has produced extensive thinking on the face as a site of human expression—from Freud, who emphasizes the face as a display of unconscious material, and Jung, who sees it as a screen for projection and imagination, to James Hillman, for whom wrinkles are expressive traces of character.

There is no other part of the body that humans need to learn to read as meticulously from an early age on. Being at once the seat of multiple senses and verbal as well as non-verbal expressions, faces are really intrafaces, connecting us to the world as an essential part of the feedback loop that is self-making and world-making. Despite our deep familiarity with the face, it holds a fascination and a mystery in the difference between inner experience and outward appearance. There is an abyss that opens up in the face of possible deception, masking for protection, and misinterpretation. In the mirror, we see it looking back at us.

So here they were, a Jewish psychoanalyst teaching a class on the connections between faces' shapes and their deeper truths, attended by a Persian photographer. The course took place in an artistic and intellectual milieu whose progressive emphasis on individual development and inner cultivation stood worlds apart from the typologies of the "criminal face" proposed by Cesare Lombroso or the measurements of National Socialist racial doctrine. Instead, it focused on the development of perception and intuition. It existed at a moment when individuality was still cultivated inwardly, before it would increasingly become legible, measurable, and governable. Its declared goal was not a classification of faces, but the cultivation of mindful observation that honors the evasive nature of the "truth" of a person.

This way of seeing was already in the process of becoming historically fragile. It was New York in 2002, and 9/11 had just begun to send its ripples out through time. In its wake, the progress in neural networks and machine learning necessary for facial recognition and mass surveillance, then only in their early stages, would be pushed on a large scale. The social understanding of what a face meant in practical and political terms was about to change dramatically in the following decades.

Face to Face with Your Own Face and the Ones That Came Before

Sahihi already found himself confronted with these practical and political terms when his family moved from Iran to Germany. He was seven years old, and the only kid in his class who looked "different." Consequently, he started thinking about the face and all it does or does not give away about the inside of a person—about the paradox it holds, of being us and still not being identical with us. About how we must come to terms with the gap of untranslatability, the permanent remainder that cannot be understood, only seen, and yet often is overlooked. His work testifies to the continuing examination of these questions. It can be read as a study of the face in its function as a place of difference and belonging. As the fascination with being inextricably tied to the "ego skin" of one's own face and its changes over time—how they are shaped by our emotions, affects, environment, and ancestry.

Ancestry and facial familiarity are at the core of Sahihi's lenticular portraits. In these family portraits, he uses a special splicing technique that allows him to superimpose multiple faces. Through a plastic lens, you can see a different face depending on the angle from which you look at the picture. These lenticular images visualize genealogies of overlapping and deviating generations, tracing heritage and personal phenomenology. Our parents' faces become the blueprint for our ways to express emotion. They also hold the deepest memories of understanding an "other" through their micro expressions and facial cues. Moreover, they play a crucial part in the foundation of understanding ourselves when our parents mirror our emotions back to us. We recognize ourselves in and through our parents' faces.

Oversight, Control, and Optimization

Genealogy and its manifestation in our faces have not only held personal but also public significance throughout history. Portraits of rulers testified to the genetic (or mythological) legitimacy of their reign. During the rise of nationalism in Europe in the nineteenth century, the face became a problematic entry point of identity and belonging, marking in-groups and out-groups. Esoteric and political worldviews were cemented with racist pseudoscience. But the desire to read the face as a bearer of truth did not disappear with the discrediting of physiognomy; it was reorganized, refined, and eventually automated.

Complex systems of measurement, categorization, and classification were developed over centuries that could not only read the faces of rulers but also those of the broader population. The evolving bio-political and economic apparatus refined and expanded these practices further, driven by the hunger for oversight, control, and optimization. On our ID, the face is being used as the primary marker for being identical to oneself when we travel.

The progression of AI technology now holds a multiplicity of ways in which the human face is being used for political control and economic extraction. The seeds for totalitarian surveillance have sprouted into monstrous flowers with beautiful names like Lavender and Palantir. While governments claim national security as the reason for implementing these technologies, our faces have become the territory of insecurity for individuals. We inhabit a reality in which we can be tracked, arrested, and sentenced wrongly because police software misidentifies our faces; in which we don't know when we are being

filmed in public, and our movements are linked to our online footprints; in which employers assess our productivity by monitoring facial expressions, and websites and platforms trace our emotional engagement to optimize advertising and attention.
Today, AI can not only identify a specific person in a large mass by their face but also markets itself as capable of reading their level of awareness, emotional state, and sexual orientation. The declared goal is to crack the materialistic code to inner experience for hermetic oversight, control, and optimization of the population. For maximal profits, the human experience must be extracted as thoroughly and completely as possible. The changing cultural significance of the face is embedded in the deep transformations of the larger social contracts.

Blurring the Lines, Softening the Borders

Gen Z, being the first generation to grow up with social media from childhood on, is aware of the gap between inner experience and the surface of identity and face. The generation that is being described as the most racially and ethnically diverse and most globally connected uses the performativity and multiplicity of social media to distort and disrupt the borders of social categories. They are used to exposing and withdrawing their private selves while simultaneously navigating surveillance and the intractable memory of the internet. They are used to experiencing their own and others' faces filtered, scored, and mediated by machines and, therefore, are highly aware of their curated artificiality. Moreover, they subvert these categories to resist their exploitation and mark their constructedness. The lines between active resistance and intuitive adaptation to their given surroundings seem to be just as fuzzy, moving, and heterogeneous. This observation of the blurring of lines of class, gender, and race is what Sahihi strives to convey in the *New York/Paris* series. While all of the historical contexts of the face reverberate throughout the portraits, they make up new interference patterns of the present. As Sahihi's work is always looking for the subversive and the borderline, the *New York/Paris* series examines Gen Z faces from contemporary metropolitan cultures. It is a generation that is renegotiating social limitations and deconstructing the promise of identity with self. It is also a generation faced with the gap between being highly connected and commodified, circulated, and controlled. In the materiality of their portrait lingers the difference between encountering a face and processing one.

Colophon

EXHIBITION
This catalogue is published in conjunction with the exhibition *ParisNewYorkPortraits* at Lea Bischofberger Gallery in Zurich, Switzerland in March 2026.

CATALOGUE
Editors: Lea Bischofberger, Ashkan Sahihi
Authors of the contributions: Sussan Babaie, Saskia Trebing, Natascha Schoenaich-Carolath, Ocean Vuong
Copyediting and proofreading: Aaron Bogart
Project management: David Fesser
Production: Amelie Solbrig
Layout and typesetting: Annette Kussin
Image processing: Jan Scheffler
Reproductions: Ul Vohrer & Annette Berr at d'mage
Printing and binding: DZA Druckerei zu Altenburg

Publishing and distribution:
Deutscher Kunstverlag
An Imprint of Walter de Gruyter GmbH
Genthiner Straße 13
10785 Berlin

ISBN 978-3-422-80428-9
Library of Congress Control Number: 2026932572

Bibliographic information published by the Deutsche Nationalbibliothek: The Deutsche Nationalbibliothek lists this publication in the Deutsche Nationalbibliografie; detailed bibliographic data are available on the Internet at http://dnb.dnb.de.

www.deutscherkunstverlag.de
www.degruyterbrill.com

Questions about General Product Safety Regulation:
productsafety@degruyterbrill.com

Allow me to say thank you.

I do not know where to begin. So much to be greatful for, so many people to thank. Of course, every single one of these beautiful humans—first in Paris, then New York— who stood in a quiet, daylight studio with me, allowed me to point the camera at those who will shape our collective future, ask them about their lives, plans, and aspirations. You all have a snug place in my heart.
The incomparable Josephine Little in Paris who knew better than I did what I meant when I talked about the beauty I see in the next generation. She brought amazing young people to the studio.
Philippe Saint Gilles for being the kind of friend everybody should have in Paris or anywhere in the world really.
Alchemist and master printer Jochen Rohner, who treats my exposed film like his own children and interprets the resulting negatives with technical sovereignty and creative finesse.
Annette Kussin for her elegant and truly extraordinary *Feingefühl* as a designer and friend.
Jan Scheffler, lithographer with two lifetimes' worth of experience and expertise. Annette Berr & Ul Vohrer of d'mage for being my trusted full support for many projects for many years.
At Deutscher Kunstverlag Kathleen Herfurth who received me with calm and grace; she knew to bring Amelie Solbrig into the team for competence in production and its flow. David Fesser for his help presenting the beautifully written contribution of beloved writer and lauded poet Ocean Vuong, much admired and celebrated Sussan Babaie of the Courtauld Institute of Art, the unerring and astute Saskia Trebing, and Natascha Schoenaich-Carolath who knows like no other to translate her academic knowledge into compassion. I cannot thank all these beautiful friends enough.
Thank you Kaveh & Cora Sheibani, words fail me here, none are big enough. Olin Roenpage in Berlin and David J. Cohen in New York City, my confidants and beacons on both sides of the big water.
Lea Bischofberger, for I love and adore her as a friend, trust and admire her as my gallerist. Thank you, Magdalena Peckskamp, for the beauty and warmth in my life.

And of course, as always, my children Jaya, Ananda, and Jake.
None of this would mean anything without their love.
May love reign supreme.

Ashkan Sahihi, London, January 2026

MIX
Paper | Supporting responsible forestry
FSC® C100411